"Mona honey,... please lift your chin a bit to the left....

... or is it a bit to the right?"

HAZY...?

CRAZY...?

and/or LAZY...?

THE MALIGNING OF CHILDREN *and adults* WITH LEARNING DISABILITIES

BY JOSEPH H. ROSENTHAL, MD, PhD.
KAISER-PERMANENTE MEDICAL CENTER
280 WEST MACARTHUR BOULEVARD
OAKLAND, CALIFORNIA 94611

International Standard
Book Number: 0-87879-058-6

Library of Congress
Catalog Card Number: 73-88784

Cover Design: James H. Wallace

This book was set in IBM Century 10 point
medium type, 10 point medium italic,
11 point Press Roman italic, and 8 point
medium italic. Chapter titles were set in
Varityper 24 point Casual Serif. The paper
used was 60 pound Arbor; for the
cover, 10 point CIS

Second Printing, 1974
Third Printing, 1982
Fourth Printing, Revised Edition, 1986.

Printed in the
United States of America

To
my patients and their parents . . .
thank you . . .
for teaching me.

FOREWORD—FOURTH PRINTING—REVISED EDITION

This Fourth Printing — Revised Edition — is the result of ---and in response to --- overwhelming numbers of requests* for new copies of Hazy? Crazy? And/Or Lazy? — The Maligning of Children (and Adults) with Learning Disabilities — because:
1. of my continued, unabated, never-ending struggle for self-aggrandizement ---
2. of my fortuitous meeting with a talented, intuitive and sensitive young artist — Karen Gassman — who drew these insightful cartoons for this Revised Edition.
3. I'm almost out of the Third Printing!

* from my wife, 3 sons, mother, mother-in-law

AFTERWORD — Dear reader, please tell your friends --- and buy copies --- and --- and --- permit me to explain ---
It's not really the money, you know ---
It's --- well --- *THE IMMORTALITY!*

Contents

Prologue

A concise overview of:

1. The child with learning disabilities,
2. The neurologically handicapped child,
3. The educationally handicapped child,
4. The child with minimal cerebral dysfunction,
5. The child with minimal brain dysfunction,
6. The child with minimal cerebral damage,
7. The child with minimal brain damage,
8. The child with developmental disorders,
9. The underachieving child,
10. The scatter-on-the-IQ-test child,
11. The child with motor-perceptual problems,
12. The child with eye-hand coordination problems,
13. The child with central nervous system integration deficits,
14. The child with large-muscle problems,
15. The child with small-muscle problems,
16. The child with intermediate(?) muscle problems,
17. The child with impaired discrimination of size problems,
18. The child with impaired discrimination of right-left problems,
19. The child with impaired discrimination of up-down problems,
20. The child with impaired discrimination of part-whole problems,
21. The child with impaired discrimination of figure-ground problems,

22. The child with soft neurological findings,

23. The hypokinetic child,

24. The hyperkinetic child,

25. The hyperactive child,

26. The clumsy child,

27. The child with impaired discrimination of auditory stimuli,

28. The child with receptive aphasic problems,

29. The child with expressive aphasic problems,

30. The child with delayed language development,

31. The child with mild hearing loss,

32. The child with mild speech irregularities,

33. The child with athetoid-choreiform movements,

34. The child with patterned movements,

35. The child with tics and grimaces,

36. The dyslexic child,

37. The dysgraphic child,

38. The dyscalculic child,

39. The child with day-to-day performance variability,

40. The child with poor work-organizing ability,

41. The child with auditory sequencing problems,

42. The child with visual sequencing problems,

43. The slow-to-finish-work child,

44. The child with poor abstract reasoning ability,

45. The child with poor attention span,

46. The distractible child,

47. The day-dreamy child,

48. The day-dreamy yet distractible child,

49. The child with poor concept formation,

50. The perseverative child,

51. The child with emotional lability,

52. The impulsive child,

53. The explosive child,

54. The child with poor impulse control,

55. The low-tolerance-for-frustration child,

56. The short-fused kid,

57. The school-problemed child with enuresis, and

58. The school-problemed child with bed-wetting,

59. The child with body and head rocking,

60. The child with poor peer relationships,

61. The child with poor social judgment,

62. The child with developmental milestone lags,

63. The child with maturational delay,

64. The immature child,

65. The socially overbold child,

66. The socially overshy child,

67. The child who does better in a 1 to 1 as opposed to a 30 to 1 relationship,

68. The child with poor short-term memory,

69. The child with poor long-term memory,

70. The child with rage reactions,

71. The child with temper tantrums,

72. The gullible and easily led child,

73. The poor-adjustment-to-change child,

74. The verbally hyperactive child,

75. The child with decreased concentration span,

76. The child with central nervous system processing dysfunction,

77. The child with school problems,

78. The child with behavior problems,

79. The child with learning disorders,

80. The dyspraxic child,

81. 2 to the 81st power because of lack of mutual exclusivity,

82. Etc., etc., etc.

Learning Disabilitologist

SELF-APPOINTED   SELF-ANNOINTED

Learning Disabilitologists

Gather About
The Flag-Escutcheon

Educators
Parents
Psychologists
Physicians
Nurses
Allied Health Professionals
Occupational Therapists
Speech & Language Specialists
Social Workers
Administrators
Probation & Justice System Personnel < Juvenile / Adult
Nutritionists
Researchers
Vocational Counselors
Rehab. Counselors
Judges ... Attorneys

Etc. ... Etc. ... Etc. ...

← clogs →
(Imported --- of course!)

KAREN GASSMAN '84

Apologies and philosophies of a Learning Disabilitologist *

I have always thought or at least wanted to think of myself as a relatively moral fellow and therefore it was not without some inner turmoil that I finally settled upon this title—Hazy . . .? Crazy . . . ? Lazy . . . ?—the maligning of children with learning disabilities. The reasons for my choice quite simply are these:

- Unfortunately, that's often how the children of the Prologue are maligned
- My almost addictive adulation for alliteration and agreeable rhyme (notice the five A's)
- Shock value to sell more copies

I was aware of previous literary successes based in part on suggestive—yea, even salacious—titles like these: "The Sayings, Playings, and Strayings of the Suburban Male," and "Every Woman Should . . . If She Could . . . But Would She Though?" Still, these books— seemingly—helped people in trouble, which is also my overwhelming, underlying motivation. No further justification was needed after this adroit, intensive rationalization, and authorship was on its way.

During my years of caring for children with school problems, each of the 82 diagnostic categories listed in the Prologue has at one time or another been presented to me. Unfortunately, several if not many of the 82 terms have been used about the same child . . . often at the same time . . . by different professionals . . . with indisputable credentials . . . suggesting different causes . . . recommending different managements . . . about the same child!

---

*Copyright pending on this neologism.

Human nature, notwithstanding its need for understanding and calm, reacted in the parents, children, and professionals involved in school problems with CONFUSION——►ANXIETY——► GUILT——►HOSTILITY——►AGGRESSION toward self and society and generally——►CHAOS!

In our clinic, children's learning problems—cognitive and behavioral—undergo extensive and intensive multidisciplined assessments including:

- A complete history—prenatal, natal, postnatal
- A complete school history
- A complete physical examination
- A complete neurological examination
- An expanded neurological examination
- A complete blood count (if indicated)
- A complete urinalysis (if indicated)
- Special blood tests (if indicated)
- Special urine tests (if indicated)
- X-rays of the head (if indicated)
- Electroencephalograms (if indicated)
- Psychoeducational testing
- Vision examination
- Hearing examination
- Long-term observation

After such assessments I used to ask the parents and the children, "Now do you understand the causes and effects and managements of the school difficulties which Johnny and Mary have?" Their answers and question-answers recurrently unnerved, rattled, and stunned me:

"Well, no, not really, Doc."
"Is it brain damage?"
"What did we do wrong?"
"Will he grow out of it?"
"Is she retarded?"
"What did we do wrong?"
"Can I punish him into sitting still?"
"Why can't I punish him into sitting still?"
"What did we do wrong?"
"So it's all psychological, is it?"
"So it's all physical, is it?"

14

"What did we do wrong?"

"How could such a problem be inherited?"

"It's not from my side of the family!"

"Well, it's not from mine!" (spouse of preceding speaker)

"What did we do wrong?"

"He's five already—why doesn't he speak like the other kids?"

"He can see and hear and talks so well—why can't he read?"

"What did we do wrong?"

"She draws so well—why can't she write?"

"If he's sluggish, how can he still be distractible?"

"What did we do wrong?"

"What did we do wrong?"

"What did we do wrong?"

It became obvious to me after several years that if at the end of fairly exhaustive evaluations, such questions and statements could still emanate from confused, anxious, and guilt-ridden parents (especially parents) then one of the main functions of the Learning Disabilitologist was not being fulfilled. That function was to *give information* in this multidisciplined, complicated, fuzzy, anxiety-provoking, guilt-producing, hostility-creating enigma—the youngster or adult with a learning problem. That I, as a bona fide Learning Disabilitologist, could give information in this area was, as it turned out, based on the enormous presumption that the information given to parents, children, and other professionals was true, correct, honest, valid, ethical, scientific, moral, clear, reliable, reasonable, rational, etc., etc., etc. (for want of space please see Section 922, page 356, of my old Thesaurus, 1941 Edition, for other equivalent terms).

My son, the doctor,
the professor,
the Learning Disabilitologist

Now comes a *very* sticky point. What gives me the right to call myself a Learning Disabilitologist? A good one, yet? Or even an adequate one? Or to start the words with capital letters, i.e., Learning Disabilitologist, implying that a defined specialty area is involved and suggesting an expertise in its title-holder? And, indeed, what are the qualifications of a Learning Disabilitologist (henceforth and forever to start with capital letters)? Where do they come from and whither go they? Will their escutcheons be greeted by joy or scorn? Forgive me, I am overwhelmed by the emotions of the moment. Learning Disabilitologists are those persons—not determined by race, sex, or creed—who comprehend, feel, sense, have a knack for assessing the subtleties and variabilities in the cognitive and behavioral performance of children (and therefore also adults). Generally their ranks, albeit small, are filled from the disciplines of education, psychology, and medicine. Yet some of the finest Learning Disabilitologists I've known have been sensitive (via being sensitized) parents who have lived through the soul-pain of raising children who were "different." Another requirement is that the Learning Disabilitologist must have some respect if not understanding of the other disciplines with which he or she must work to formulate a complete and comprehensible diagnosis, story, evaluation—so that the organic and emotional components of the problems of a child with school difficulties are crystallized as clearly as possible. In this way, all involved will know what to worry about. But perhaps more importantly, they will be relieved of unnecessary worry, fear, anxiety, guilt, and hostility.

This brings us to a triage type of philosophy which is one of the guiding principles of the Kaiser-Permanente Medical Center at Oakland, California.* Historically, man has tended to divide himself according to various models:

optimists—pessimists

boys—girls

the good—the bad

leftists—rightists

religionists—atheists

etc., etc., etc.,

Our group has subdivided humanity, via a new paradigm, into three subgroups:

the sick

the well

the concerned well

(or the well concerned, depending on how one looks at it). The sick are the simplest group, relatively speaking, to care for. Fractured bones, strep throats, bee bites, and poison oak mandate, *usually* definitive treatment patterns. The well, we would like to keep well—by appropriate preventive procedures to anticipate and remediate disease processes in their initial stages when they are amenable to early intervention. Ah, but the concerned well—this is a group burdened by worries, fears, and anxieties to which they have no right, people who are perhaps not focused enough on more pressing if not obvious problems.

The ambiguities which unglue the concerned well—usually the parents, often the children, and also professionals involved in learning problems—stem from several sources. The one I have mentioned above as the first great challenge to the Learning Disabilitologist is the lack of information in this fuzzy area. The second problem has to do with the multiplicity of data—collated from various sources . . . often contradictory . . . and rigidly interpreted by the professionals of the disciplines involved.

When there are many different ways to "fix" something (a child or an adult with a learning problem), ways that are based on different evaluations of the causes and effects of that trouble, then confusion ———→ consternation———→ chaos. Especially in the families of the children with learning problems. In most disciplines the "I-don't-want-to-take-off-my-blinders" syndrome is usually related directly to the number of years since the degree, certificate, or statement of competency was granted. There seems to

---

Greer Williams, Kaiser-Permanente Health Plan—Why It Works (Oakland, California: The Henry J. Kaiser Foundation, 1971).

be an unwillingness in some professionals as they get older—and presumably wiser—to allow apparently reasonable, relevant, and reliable information to upset their cognitive set. Because, quite frankly, thinking (especially thinking about contradictory data) is work. It's hard work, and if the new data suggest that one might have been wrong all along it's unnerving work—and who needs that when things were going along so well . . . that raise, that new title, that new car, or the Van Gogh (original, of course), etc., etc., etc. Before my supporters suggest sainthood, and my detractors cry "hypocrisy," permit me to say that I too have been possessed, but lately not so much, by this demon.

That the data pertaining to learning problems can come from specialists from A to Z has finally been proved without a shadow of a doubt by the following table:

A. Audiologist
B. Brain-Wave Doctor *or*
   Biochemist
C. Child Psychologist
D. Developmental Specialist
E. Emotional-Cause-at-the-Root-of-All-Problems Specialist
   or
   Endocrinologist
F. Friend-Next-Door-Who-Raised-Twelve-of-Her-Own
G. Group-Encounter-Discussion Leader *or*
   Geneticist
H. Handicapped Children's Specialist
I. Intelligence Tester
J. Job Training Specialist
K. Kindergarten Retention Discussor
L.
M. Mother-in-Law *or*
   Medicine-Is-the-Answer-for-All-Problems Specialist *or*
   Mental Health Specialist
N. Neurologist
O. Ophthalmologist *or*
   Occupational Therapist *or*
   Organic-Cause-at-the-Root-of-All-Problems Specialist
P. Pediatrician *or*
   Psychologist *or*
   Perceptual Motor Specialist *or*
   Psychometrist *or*
   Pharmacologist

Q. Quack—Out-and-Out Quack

R. Reading Specialist

S. Sigh-chiatrist (sorry, I couldn't resist this one) *or*
Speech and Language Specialist *or*
Social Worker

T. Teacher

U. Uninvited Guest (opinions, diagnoses, referrals over coffee or tea)

V. Vision Muscle Exercise Specialist

W. Wednesday's Issue of That Ladies' Magazine with the Article-with-All-the-Answers

X. X-Rays-of-the-Head Specialist

Y. You

Z. Zoologists, Zebrists, and Zeusists (the philosophy which maintains that because of evolution directly from zebra to man, all human behavior and mental function problems are due to a misalignment of the black and white stripes and that only Zeus knows how to fix them)

The careful reader will surely have noted that L is blank. The reason of course, is that L stands for Learning Disabilitologist—the final word, the discipline of disciplines, the specialty of specialties in this problem area.

As a specialty, Learning Disabilitology contradicts its etymology. (This last sentence . . . it rhymes . . . it sings.) Specialty derives from special, which derives from a Latin root meaning "individual" or "particular." Most specialties and subspecialties cone down on more individual aspects of general subjects. For example: *coprolalologists* (those who study only dirty words) and *sinistre simianologists* (those who study only the left hands of apes).

To dispel my readers' suspicions that increasing specialization is a function of modern times, allow me to let you in on a very old joke from Babylonian days. One feller meets another feller near the ziggurat and says, "Say, what d'you do for a living?" The other feller says, "I'm an eye doctor." The first feller chortles, "Which eye?"

Well, anyway, Learning Disabilitology is a specialty which by its nature must fan out rather than cone down. The true Learning Disabilitologist must respect, appreciate, and have some knowledge of the other 25-35 alphabetized disciplines listed above. He or she must be a core professional who, as I see it, has two outstanding duties:

- To give information in a fuzzy area

- To integrate all the pertinent data so that they make a comprehensible livable-with unity for the child and parents and professionals involved in the turmoil surrounding a child with problems in school.

And these two duties are exactly what this book is about. What this book is *not* meant to be is:

- An exhaustive volume with full bibliography encompassing the historical background, research areas, and managements of children and adults with learning difficulties. (In other words, this is not a textbook.)

- A definitive expostulation that there is only one real truth about learning difficulties. (We know too little at this time to have the final truth. Actually, do we ever really know that much in any field?)

Oh, yes—one more important aim of this book is to give pleasurable reading time. I consider reading as a personal interaction between reader and author. I want to bring joy into this relationship because, quite frankly, then I get pleasure from it as well. I give a little piece of my mind, my humor, my soul in each chapter. But if I succeed in my aims, then my mind, my humor, my soul grow. And so I can give more later on.

This feeling I have is based on an old Jewish proverb, "Gib a guten Vort," which literally means "Give a good word." (There I've let it slip out and I'm sure you never would have guessed.) Life-style proverbs are funny. I suspect that some folks look for one that sounds right and then try to mold their sayings and doings about it—even though their first reactions might tend to be in the opposite direction. Anyway, for me, after having felt this way for as long as I can remember, I found the proverb for the feeling. "Give a good word" further means that in one's interaction with another in the point-counterpoint of life—"Be a nice guy." . . . "Make the other guy happy." . . . "Make him smile." . . . "What could it cost you? And even if it did, so what?" Life is so hectic, complicated, organized, and disorganized that a word, a smile, a joke—a good word, a good smile, a good joke—can do wonders, I feel. (Forgive me for the philosophy—but who knows when I'll get another publisher?)

A few pages back, I introduced the concept of my perhaps dubious right to call myself a Learning Disabilitologist. (False modesty, to be sure, but good for a few tugs at the professional heartstrings.) I had fantasized that colleagues, confreres, and even creditors would hasten to write those grandiloquent fly-leaf introductions. But suddenly they were all gone. Professor Charley went on a sudden expense-free trip to the headwaters of the Volga. Dr. John is incommunicado, celebrating his two-and-a-half-year anniversary. Of what? For four weeks? Straight? This other friend said, "Joe *who* is calling?" And so, dear reader, you must turn to the next chapter for qualifications and self-endorsements.

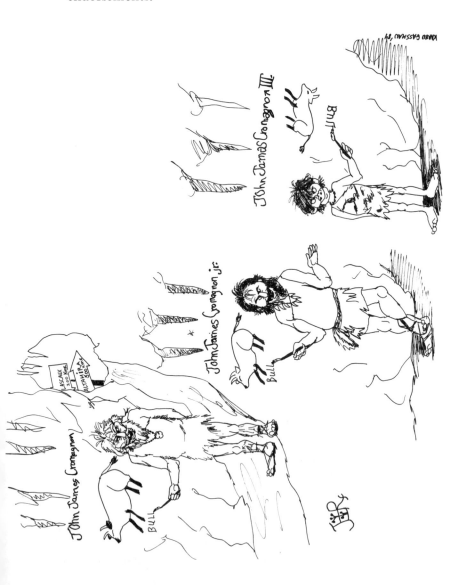

The difference between "different" and different

Why can't she and he
  Be just like thee and me?
So that the family of humanity
  Would be like we?
    Only we!
Or else . . . baby! *

As Director of the Learning Disabilities Clinic of the Department of Pediatrics at the Kaiser Permanente Medical Center at Oakland, California, I have known some 1100 youngsters and adults with school problems. Directly and indirectly, but mostly directly, I have known their parents, their siblings, their peers, and involved professionals.

Originally trained as a pediatrician, I was introduced to the practical aspects of child development—to its vagaries, vicissitudes, and variabilities—by my own three children, and was given succor and suggestions through the years by the two great intuitive clinicians of my time—my wife and my mother.

Having met, examined, spoken with, listened to, managed the treatment of, and I hope—I so hope—understood these 1100 children and adults, several global conclusions became manifest:

- As individuals they are not *so* different yet "different" from their "normal" peers
- As individuals they are not *so* different yet "different" from one another

These are the stunning observations of so many years of clinical expertise and research? (This interrogative sentence should be

---

*From the "Worticisms and Farcetiae of John James Cromagnon." (It was that way even then, baby.)

read with a lot of rising intonation, preferably with a New York accent. Actually, it should be read out loud. Actually, even more, I think my reader would better enjoy the book if all the sentences were sort of read out loud. And then, all through the community, there would be heard a ringing chorus—unless of course different readers were at different parts of the book at the same time. Then it would be a wringing chorus. I'm sorry, I couldn't resist that one.)

Allow me to parenthetically, almost pathetically but not pathologically, add that the study of the subtleties of cognitive and behavioral malfunctioning was by no means defined into a professional discipline until relatively recently. When I was in medical school—lo, these many years ago—we touched on the subjects in neurology, psychiatry, pediatrics, and in the philosophy of human development but I never had to study for or worry about or receive a grade in the minimal cerebral dysfunctions.

One crux of the problems of these individuals is that they are "different" not different from their "normal" (whatever that might mean) peers. Different is easy to deal with because the lines are relatively clear:

righteous—evil

healthy—sick

intelligent—retarded

great athlete—cerebral palsied

sharp-eyed—blind

great ear for rhythm—deaf

attractive—malformed

complete self-control—epileptic

Ah, but "different" is quite different from different you see, because the quotation marks imply lack of definition, uncertainty, malingering, or even fraud. The 1100 patients are of all ages, ethnic groups, and physical appearances. They are of both sexes but boys predominate (we can go into the reasons for this later on). Their "differences" from "normal" peers and among themselves are noted in the great variety and variability of their weaknesses and strengths in academic and/or behavioral functioning in school and/or at home.

Yet there are subtle underlying bonds which tend to cluster them into a descriptive subgroup of our general population—unfortunately a misunderstood and maligned subgroup.

- They can all usually see well . . .
- They can all usually hear well . . .
- They are all usually in possession of good or even super-good intelligence . . . if . . . if . . . if . . . they are approached only by certain interactional means and not by others.

To be more specific, there are divergences in their talents, discrepancies in their capacities, and disparities in their accomplishments—without a scientific explanation or even a good reason or even a tenable hypothesis (until recently of course).

I'm talking about John, who is 16 years old, handsome, and a great basketball player. But John has trouble with essay questions on tests. He often knows the answers and does well in true-false or multiple-choice tests. Why then can't he put his thoughts on paper? He's putting us on! Or is he? He's poorly motivated—probably relying on his athletic talents to get by. But why trouble just with essays? Dysgraphia? What's that?

I'm talking about Mary, who is 10 years old, charming, bright, pretty, and talkative. But Mary refuses (?) or can't seem to follow a series of verbal instructions.

Vignette

Adult or peer (smiling): "Mary, please close the door, open the window, feed the cat, and do your homework."

Mary (after having closed the door) (looking nonplussed): "What was that again?"

Adult or peer (scowling): "What's the matter with you, Mary? Are you deaf or dumb or being recalcitrant?" (No one would ever really say "recalcitrant" in parlour conversation but you get the idea, I'm sure.)

Mary (nervous, moving to center stage and then with a brave toss of her little head): "Well, no, I'm not deaf or dumb or whatever that other word means. Dr. Rosenthal thinks I might have auditory sequencing difficulties!" (Curtain falls. Audience cries: "Author! Author!")

I'm talking about Jimmie, who is 6½ years old, cute, alert, and smart. But you can sure see the discipline problems in that family. Jimmie refuses to sit still. He's constantly in motion. He jumps up and down and tears up our new couch (you know, the one we got on sale because of that mild shipping damage) each time he comes to our house. His parents are in group counseling

but it doesn't seem to help Jimmie yet. You know . . . sometimes
. . . I think . . . he can't help moving about so much. Is that possible? I mean, could it be physical in some way? But how could
it be? So that's what hyperactive means?

I'm talking about Mr. Smith, who is 35 years old, a loving
husband, and a great father. He's a master mechanic, Doc, and
with time-and-a-half almost makes as much as you do, Doc, and
you know, Doc (the Ha Ha of weak laughter is heard) how much
that is. But you know, I just found out that he can't read! No,
really. He just barely gets by headlines and the sports pages.
Pictures help him a lot and his wife has to help him with spelling
—almost like he was a little kid. Isn't it amazing that such a *retarded person* could *manipulate* his life *so cleverly* that no one
knew he couldn't read till now? (Dear reader, please, please read
this last sentence over again.)

I'm talking about Billy, who is 5 years old and cannot speak
in full sentences yet. He'll be in kindergarten next fall, you know.
Not enough environmental stimulation, I guess. His parents probably don't have enough time to talk with him because they read
too much. You know, those cool, stand-offish intellectual types.
What's that you say? They do talk to him a lot? Oh, well, then
they probably say the wrong things. Anyway, it sounds like a
mental problem to me.

I'm talking about Dick, who is 17 years old and in Juvenile
Hall. He seems to learn quite well by listening or by pictures, and
speaks clearly. Why can't he read past the third grade level? And
his spelling is a joke. His parents used to read to him when he
was about a year old. Did they push him so hard that he tuned
out on reading? Only reading and spelling, though! His math is
fine, or rather was fine, as were other school subjects. Just that
reading and spelling! Can you really—from a psychological point
of view—just selectively tune out one area of learning? Was it because his parents forced the reading? I suppose it's possible but
it's not logical to me. You know, actually, only his mother used
to read to him. Yes, yes, that's right—only his mother. Because . . .
I remember now, his father had the same trouble in reading and
spelling too. And you know, he has two first cousins, both boys,
on his father's side who visited from the East last year—they have
the same trouble! I wonder, could this reading and spelling problem be passed on in the family in some way? You know, by
genetics or heredity? That's really spooky—if that could be so.
But colorblindness and that blood disease, hemophilia, are inher-

ited—so why not. . . . What's that you call it, Doc? Dyslexia! Dyslexia?

Or does Dick have the reading and spelling problem because he didn't get enough phonics from his first grade teacher? You remember that Mrs. Jones. That pretty one with those modern ideas about teaching reading by sight-see as well as by phonics. And that business about the half day for structured learning and the other half day for creativity. . . . Well, you know, she finally did get divorced.

But it's hard to understand about Dick. Why should he end up in Juvenile Hall? He was such a sweet boy. Never got into trouble. Always helped his folks about the house and yard. But that reading business finally got to him, I guess.

Some people called him stupid, retarded, MR, and hazy!

Some people called him poorly motivated, idle, and lazy!

Some people called him psychopathologic, abnormal, and crazy!

These people included peers, even family members, and even some professionals. After a while, Dick couldn't help thinking poorly of himself. His self-concept and self-esteem dipped lower and lower. "If all these people think I'm hazy, crazy, and/or lazy, I guess I must be," he often cried himself to sleep. "Well, if I'm bad like they all say I am, I might as well act bad," he sorrowed. That's when the clown and show-off behavior started. You know, like taking any dare. Like walking on the window ledges of buildings. And then came the lying and the stealing, and Juvenile Hall.

And I'm talking about Susan, who is 12 years old and always spilling, tripping, and clinging. She's so pretty, and yet there's something missing. Most people think she's quite a character. In kindergarten, the milk and cookies almost always ended up by her ears or in her hair instead of in her mouth. It's almost as if she didn't know where her arm ended and her body began. Even now, she can't tell right from left at times. But all her vision tests are normal, I'm told. And she's always falling over her feet! But she's not weak at all. Her muscles are quite strong. She just cannot learn to knit, and dancing lessons are a torture for her. I guess that even though her muscles are sturdy she can't get them to work one with another. Is that possible? You mean there *is* a difference between strength and coordination? It certainly shows in her swimming. Susan just can't get it all together. And, oh, does she lean on you! Always touching you and hanging on . . . it's almost like she doesn't know where she is in space or where she ends and you begin. Well, anyway, with this behavior she'll certainly get into trouble with the boys in a few years. I wonder why she's like that? Is she so emotionally insecure that she has to hang on to people physically? Or . . . or . . . are there physical reasons like figure-ground or part-whole or left-right discrimination problems? But that's so fuzzy an answer! Oh, come on, Doc, what do you mean "soft" neurological signs? Really, Doc!

etc.   etc.   etc.

The common denominator among these eight problemed people is almost the absence of a common denominator, yet a fine but finite thread links them into an almost amorphous amalgamative archetype. To shed light I will strive to:

1. Get rid of the "almost"
2. Add body to the "amorphous"
3. Define and explain the "amalgamatives"
4. Establish with understanding and, I hope, compassion the "archetype" of the minimal cerebral dysfunctions within the framework of psychobiological development

And for this, dear reader, we must turn to the next chapter.

The continuum
of psychobiological development
or
Folks are generally
a bit more alike than different

When I was a young man ("Oh, but you still are!" the nurses laughingly but alas, not longingly, chirp) I was constantly intrigued by the enigma of how one distinguishes a qualitative from a quantitative difference. At college we used to sit around with new pipes in our mouths (that was "in" then), the smoke getting in each other's eyes, lungs, and pastrami sandwiches (very hot mustard and Yenem's Pipe Mixture did wild things to my cognitive functioning then) and ponder the great mystery . . . *how much different does different have to be to make it a qualitative rather than a quantitative difference?* Actually the only reason I used to smoke a pipe was to fill the emptiness left by a missing right upper canine until the permanently placed prosthesis finally arrived. Ah, vanity, vanity . . . thou belongest not to woman alone. I finally approached a great professorial mind later in my life and asked the question: "When does a difference in degree become a difference in kind?" The profound professorial principle, after but a few moments of mental musing, was this: "When the extrinsic difference is so great that it becomes an intrinsic difference!" A stunning, classic interpretation! Of circular reasoning! The final tautology!

I thought on, bravely, by myself and as I got on in years it seemed that previously clear and opposite polarities of positions, premises, and polemics were liquefying into more variable, subtle, complex, and changeable intermedia (a sparkling neologism on literature's vista). I find it increasingly difficult to say always or never . . . indicate absolutely right or incontrovertibly wrong . . .

diagnose the purest of good or the basest of evil—unless of course I become tired, upset, or angry. But when these emotional states do occur, are they not accompanied by a loss of a bit of one's rationality? I think so. And I strongly suspect the same might be true of other folks as well.

Notice: Watch out, reader! I think that this author is setting you up for the trap and dogma of *relativism.*

Those who argue for individual and group differences—for example, in culture, language, and personality—and I think I'm getting less and less to be one of them . . . do not, I feel, endanger the conceptual framework of the Continuum of Psychobiological Development . . . because I hypothesize that the differences . . . albeit present, prominent and even pervasive . . . *are seen more in means, methods, and machinations than in ends and effects.* These ends or needs seem to be pretty much the same for all cultural groups: biological needs . . . social needs . . . individual needs . . . and those needs which pertain to lechery, lewdness, licentiousness, lasciviousness, and libidinousness especially noted in dirty old and middle-aged men. I know I'm touching on pretty heady and even tangential stuff now but who knows when I'll get another publisher?

> When I have Fears That My Publisher May Cease to Be...
> Before Our Contract Has Cleaned My Teeming Brain...

> To be semi serious for a while, when considering ends not means, is there really a difference in kind rather than in degree between the classically labeled and libeled *materialist* who plunks down $10,000 in cash for that 645 horsed, all-powered chartreuse and lilac motorized behemoth . . .

> the urbane *sophisticate* who gently nudges his $10,000 personal check on the upper right-hand corner of the dealer's desk for that exquisite, signed, original-by-you-know-whom blank canvas entitled cleverly "Blank Canvas or Before the Thought Came To Me" . . .

> and the devout *collector* of whatever media are involved who tremulously posts the money order for $10,000 to to Southeast Parthia for the only missing piece in his legendary amassment of . . . in this case . . . Neanderthal soft drink bottle caps?

The ways and means are different in the examples cited above. Yet the underlying bond of brotherhood seems to be in their never-ending struggle for acquisitive self-aggrandizement . . . the common end.

Geographically based personality differences noted by tired, taunted, trifled-with, and taken tourists have been the subject of stories which have become legion, even though we, as a traveling family, have been warmly welcomed too. The styles and graces of these touristic trials and tribulations may have varied from place to place but the end points (ouch!) felt much the same.

In Country A I confirmed my flight twice. Got the names of the confirmers. Got to the airport quite early. Still got bumped with my family (total five). Had a temper tantrum in three languages. Was reassured that all would be OK. Rode in a small 1936 taxi. With my Lawfully-Wedded, my lineage (three boys), and my luggage in lap . . . *my* lap. For 249 kilometers (that's right, folks). To a connecting flight. With a taxi-driver who knew he was not going to be tipped.

In Country B we had First Class train tickets. After half an hour en route, I saw we were in a Second Class car. You know, by the nameplate in front of the train car up high. I asked the conductor to be conducted to the First Class car. He said there wasn't any! I insisted on a refund. "Are you kidding?" sounds the same in all languages. But I persisted that morally and according to our tickets, my family should be in a First Class car. The locals on the train were attentive. My wife questioned my ability to run the family. My three boys (each with varying versions of unresolved Oedipal Complexes) quickly agreed. The conductor saw a way out for all of us! With a great flourish, he merely, swirlingly, twirled that little handle that changed the nameplates at the top-front of the car—*from second to first class!* The locals roared.

To this day, I'm not really sure how I came out. You should hear the stories I've got for Countries C to Z. Maybe in another book someday? Please ask.

Now, I'm sure that there must be many bright PhD candidates all over the country who can deluge me with statistically significant cross-cultural data proving that all Homo sapiens are either really more alike or more different depending, of course, on how the t-tests or chi-squares came out. But to pull the whole idea together again, dear reader, I'm suggesting that when it comes to the basic and important stuff in life—ends not means (and I am not saying that ends justify means)—the family of man shows more similarities than differences.

Permit me the final expression . . . the pièce de résistance (you've got to use a sprinkling of French here and there for cultural background reasons) of the notion that seemingly divergent groups can come really close to one another in certain situations when basics are involved.

Vignette

It was May of 1953—three months before I was to enter the United States Army as a medical officer (oh, have I got stories about those two years!). It was my night off and I was on my way to the Palladium Ballroom on Broadway and about 52nd Street. As my Powerglide (to this day, I can't use my right arm and left leg in unison—no, no, not what you think) Chevrolet momboed happily and hoppily (give gas! give gas! let up—give gas! It's sort of an off-beat rhumba) to the rhythm of Tito Puente and his orchestra on the radio . . . a Spanish-language commercial intervened extolling the virtues of a certain alcoholic beverage: "EL VINO MAS BUENO DE TODO EL MUNDO, QUE ES M-A-N-I-S-C-H-E-W-I-T-Z." The millennium had come. Humanity was one. But sweet Carmen, who had taught me Spanish, was still forbidden to me.

That humanity is a continuum from a psychobiological as well as from a psychophilological point of view is seen in the following figure. This analogy stressing that we're a bit more alike than different is, I feel, valid. Unfortunately, proofs are more anecdotal than experimentally designed and more sensed than unimpeachably measured. But such is the nature of any subtlety as an old academic confrere of mine once described it: "Id don't come up and rap yu rite in da mout!" (rhymes with *out*—a quaint quasimalarticulation common to inhabitants of the southernmost part of the State of New York). If the subtleties of minimal malfunctioning in cognitive and behavioral development were not just those—subtleties—then these malfunctionings would lend themselves to relatively easy estimation, measurement, proof, reverification, categorization, and almost smug definitive definition. Such, of course, and sadly, is not the case.

My reader will note that on the far right of Figure 1 is the idealized zenith of physical, mental, and emotional impeccability which is personified in the perfections of my Lawfully-Wedded. Unfortunately, as noted on the far left of Figure 1—and it is not necessarily an indication of my political posture that all the troubles are to the left—for thousands of years we have been quite aware of some rather marked, definite, clearly diagnosible deviations from the perfect state. Generally these can be identified as the cerebral palsies, epilepsies, mental retardations, and peripheral sensory losses (blindness and deafness).

Figure 1

Continuum of Psychobiological Development

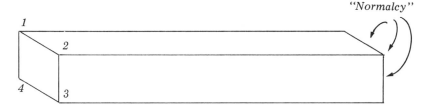

1. *Cerebral palsies*

2. *Epilepsies*

3. *Mental retardations*

4. *Peripheral sensory losses (blindness, deafness)*

Several points should be made. To adequately understand these four entities would take at least four textbooks and a great deal of sensitive clinical experience. Yet, we may attempt to define them . . . which is difficult because different disciplines in-involved in a diagnosis and direction in these problem areas might and often do define them differently from one another. I had two choices:

1. To define rigidly and get letters of complaint!
2. Or to define loosely and get letters of complaint!

Generally and globally speaking, the "cerebral palsies" comprise those abnormalities wherein voluntary control is lost in part or fully over motor or muscle functions in certain parts of the body, i.e., legs, arms, and/or head—the latter situation at times resulting in inarticulate speech (dysarthria). The causes have to do with some brain (cerebrum) disorder. They might have occurred before, during, or after birth and possible causative factors might have to do with genetics, biochemistry, infection, trauma, and/or poisoning. The two main clinical examples of the cerebral palsies are the spastic types which often result in contractures and the athetoid types wherein slow, changing, movable spasms are noted in the body.

The "epilepsies" pertain to usually chronic disorders characterized by recurring seizures or fits in which consciousness may be partly or fully lost. These attacks may be associated with tonic or clonic muscle spasms. Various clinical types of seizures have been described through the centuries among which are grand mal, petit mal, Jacksonian, and psychomotor—the latter at times manifesting behavioral aberrations. Often the electroencephalogram shows a characteristic pattern that corresponds with a definitive clinical picture.

The "mental retardations" refer to those conditions of incomplete development of mental functions, which vary quantitatively and qualitatively, but as a result of which the affected are not capable of assuming those responsibilities expected of a socially adequate person. The measurement aspects of the problem can be overwhelming, especially with the considerations of cultural, ethnic, and language backgrounds. We could spend several years discussing the IQ and its tests as well as the legal guardianship and educational ramifications of the problems of the mentally retarded. We could also spend years discussing the meanings of "development," "mental," "retardation," "capable," "responsibilities," and "socially adequate person."

The blind and the deaf *seem* relatively clear-cut as to what diagnostic criteria are involved in these disabilities. There are legal and educational definitions. Above all, I feel that adequate testing in these areas is requisite in the full assessment of those who are having school difficulties. Then we get into some interdisciplinary problems relating to vision and perception and hearing and auditory discrimination which I will touch on later.

Unfortunately, these four problem areas are not mutually exclusive. By this I mean that it is heart-rending enough to be afflicted by one of these four disabilities, but it is all the more cataclysmic to be oppressed by more than one:

to be retarded and palsied . . .
to be epileptic and retarded . . .
to be blind and retarded . . .
to be deaf, blind, and palsied . . .

But contrariwise! If one is epileptic, he is by no means necessarily also retarded. If one is palsied, she is by no means necessarily epileptic. If one is retarded, he or she is by no means necessarily also epileptic or palsied. If one is deaf or blind, he or she is by no means necessarily also retarded.

The implication is that although similarities via same diagnoses exist in these patients, all aspects of management—educational, psychological, and medical—must be individualized to fit their unique needs. And I haven't even mentioned differences in their ethnic, cultural, language, family, and economic backgrounds. I remember this one great lady, the mother of one of my boy patients. He has cerebral palsy . . . arm, leg, and speech involved. This lady enhanced every bit of talent which nature left intact in that youngster. Sometimes I think she even mended some broken nerves. She so structured his home and school environments with emotional support and material aids as to get the most from him and for him, and also a little bit for the rest of us too. Of course, the father, brothers, sisters, and teachers also helped. His mother tried all sensory avenues, in all combinations, to determine how he could learn best and most easily. For motor weaknesses, she contrived mechanical gadgets so that he could get his ideas out. This youngster has cerebral palsy; he is not retarded and he'd like to let the world know this. A great, great lady!

Even though these four problems in development are biochemically, organically, neurologically, electrophysiologically, and physically based—acknowledging that we might not often be able to pinpoint a specific cause in each case—many secondary psychologically, environmentally, analytically, Freudianly, and emotionally based sequelae can and do occur to share in the overwhelmingness of the total life-pictures of patients with these maladies.

Epilepsy, possibly, is as bad semantically as it is scientifically. The epilepsies comprise several disease states, not one, and the term is almost an evil one because its connotative ramifications conjure up visions which have rational qualifications—at times somewhat below the level of Grade D movie plots. Lack of understanding of the epilepsies leads to misunderstanding—as is probably the case in many diseases and other conditions. Giving information is thus a most important aspect of total care. Convulsive tendencies, seizure disorder, and fits in increasing order of semantic weight still do not convey the emotional tonnage on a person (and his family) who has "epilepsy." The fears which some epileptics have—that they might at any time, despite presumably good medical control, suffer a seizure—are pressures enough. But when the dark clouds of the environment—often an inadequately informed and therefore a suspicious, intolerant, and even hostile environment—are added to these burdens, life can be most un-nerving and unpleasant.

The cerebral palsies—whether linked to definitive prenatal, perinatal, or postnatal causes or to unknown causes—certainly are clinically striking:

a little boy swinging one leg with a spastic gait while holding his arm tight unto himself . . .

a little girl with slow, uncontrolled muscle movements of her hands and arms . . .

a bright-eyed youngster with badly articulated and deficient speech and language patterns.

I have seen compassion well up in the eyes and souls of par-ents and children when these patients with cerebral palsy come into our waiting rooms. These children and adults with neuro-muscular dysfunctions have to learn to live with the emotional as well as the physical components of their lives.

That the blind and the deaf must have psychological prob-lems in a world of five senses is fairly clear, I think. But to really comprehend the nature and extent of their sensations . . . I feel that we'd have to live a bit of their lives ourselves. When I tried for a while to get about without using my eyes or ears and when I could regain those functions by merely removing the eye patches or cotton ear plugs . . . then those really big problems about that costing too much and about dropping and breaking this . . . suddenly shrank in importance.

Although youngsters ·who are retarded are often grouped educationally and socially, I'm sure they can't help noticing inter-mittent quizzical looks, annoyed faces, or at times outright irrita-bility from the environment. A retarded youngster can also get emotionally upset. Which brings us to:

How retarded does one have to be to be retarded?

How cerebral palsied does one have to be to be cerebral palsied?

How epileptic does one have to be to be "epileptic"?

How blind or deaf does one have to be to be blind or deaf? (There are legal definitors in this group.)

The concept of the continuum of function⟶dysfunction exists even within the framework of these four well-established, historically clear and relatively undisputed diagnostic groups.

Johnny's "funny" walk might—around kindergarten time, by an astute clinician—be assessed as due to a *very mild* spastic gait and a *very minimally* tightened heel cord. If stretching exercises were found to be enough to correct the tight heel cord . . . would it necessarily be a good idea . . . in the long run . . . to tell Johnny, his parents, siblings, friends, foes, future associates and employers that Johnny . . . probably . . . really had such a mild case of that dreaded cerebral palsy, that almost nobody picked it up? Giving information is a most important aspect of total care . . . but information has to be given with care.

Sally's unusual but recurrent abdominal pains turned out to be a rare form of that feared disease epilepsy. The medication did help to control them. Environment thinking out loud: "But now everyone knows that Sally has abdominal epilepsy . . . and it *is* a form of real epilepsy. Isn't that so, Doc?"

Can you *over*-help people sometimes?

There is a wide range of retardation and therefore a wide range of ability within the group known as the mentally retarded. The closer one is to "normal" or "average" (whatever that may be), I suspect, the greater is one's realization that he is different . . . viewed differently and grouped differently by society. The distinction between small and large intergroup differences has continually filled me with awe. It has always seemed to me that small differences cause more problems amongst groups than do large differences. When the boy next to you is really way out from accepted local norms (as long as he's not causing patent physical or philosophical danger to the community) . . . you seem to look at him as almost culturally odd-ballish. I mean what's the point in all those anthropology, archaeology, sociology, and psychology courses we took if we can't understand (and tolerate) that far-away cultural groups can and do develop their own distinctive social patterns. But when the guy next to you is doing something just a teeny-weeny, itsy-bitsy differently from you . . . wow! It's not culturally interesting anymore; its culturally threatening. How anthropologically unusual and distinct is the Shaman-of-This-Island's treatment of appendicitis with rattles; and how melodic are the incantations of the Witch-Doctor-of-That-Peninsula for coronary thromboses. But Aesculapius forbid that two physicians in the same community should prescribe differently for colds or poison oak.

It always cracks me up how clothing for school kids has to be "just that way." Suddenly, it's this jacket or these jeans or those sneakers . . . only *this*, *that*, or *those* . . . and if a kid deviates from the "in thing" . . . anathema! How do these new styles get started in the first place? In my fantasy, I have often seen very short, thin, beardless, adult, manufacturers' representatives smuggled into schoolyards and masquerading as children. They assume the contented airs of fulfilled accomplishment and joy: chewing the right gum . . . possessing the latest orthodontic devices . . . quoting ribaldry, appropriate for age and class. . . . And of course they just happen to be wearing that garment which is to be the new-cannot-do-without-fashion: . . . zeppelin sneakers for that really airy jump in basketball . . . that *very* printed map and place-name shirt for ready help in geography tests . . . and that new rage for first graders, the ten-fingered glove set called the "math tutor". . . .

It seems that folks often fuss, fume, and fight more over ritualistic trappings and trimmings than over fundamentals.

I have not even discussed the patients who are primarily emotionally disturbed or the serious differences of opinion about whether these illnesses are essentially due to psychogenic and/or physiological causes. This would take several books.

But now we come to a group of youngsters and adults who do not fit any of the relatively clearly defined groups discussed above, but who do have problems in behavior and/or thinking so that they do not mesh with the conceptualization of a person being either all OK or all not OK. When subtleties, nonconformities, malthinkings, and apparent misbehaviors enter into the cognitive and action models of seemingly OK people . . . and the scientific-diagnostic-understanding explanations for the above are not clear . . . then we come upon that group with minimal cerebral dysfunctioning—a group misunderstood and miscalled as hazy, crazy, and/or lazy.

Definitions . . . derivations . . . and digressions or Certain ground rules to help unground certain other ground rules by

I am not by nature an innovator, adventurer, or environmental wave-maker. Quotes my Lawfully-Wedded: "At times, he's dull!" E.g., we drink bottled water and engage in elaborate hand-washing ceremonies when we travel. And when I was an adolescent . . . at neighborhood dances . . . I spent so much time figuring out who belonged with whom . . . that before I knew it . . . they were playing "Good Night Sweetheart." Invariably, the sweetheart was not me. And once on a magnificent morning at Kaanapali, Maui . . . my Lawfully-Wedded in an outburst of togetherness . . . yearned for a jog (not jug or jag) with me on the beach. . . . I mused and retorted with great urbanity: "So who'll watch the traveler's checks?" We jogged. She won. I was held back by my little KLM flight bag which flapped as I flopped. The traveler's checks were inside.

And so, dear reader, realizing what sort I am (please, no descriptions or epithets now) . . . you can, I'm sure, understand how much safer I'd feel on the firmer ground of a definition of the essence of this book at about this place in our history.

The definition of minimal cerebral dysfunction which I feel most comfortable with and which I use most frequently is taken from a monograph published by the United States Department of Health, Education, and Welfare (1966). It is phase one of a three-phase project entitled *Minimal Brain Dysfunction in Children*, edited by Sam D. Clements, PhD, and it states on page 9 . . .

MINIMAL BRAIN OR CEREBRAL
DYSFUNCTION SYNDROME DEFINITION

The term "Minimal Brain Dysfunction Syndrome" refers to children [and adults] of near average, average, or above average general intelligence with certain learning [and] or behavioral disabilities ranging from mild to severe, which are associated with deviations of function of the central nervous system. These deviations may manifest themselves by various combinations of impairment in perception conceptualization, language, memory, and control of attention, impulse or motor function.

I have taken the liberty of adding the bracketed words "and adults" and "and". My reasons, which I hope will become clearer as the book progresses, are to start with these. (Actually, if I don't make some changes, the status of my expertise might be questioned.) If, in fact, we do not find minimal cerebral dysfunctionings *per se* in adults, it might well be because these adults have managed either to compensate for or to hide these difficulties in various ways through the years:

An adolescent with small-muscle problems becomes a PhD in 12th century Middle European obscenities rather than a diamond cutter . . .

An adolescent with expressive language problems becomes a highly salaried hitting outfielder rather than a politician . . .

An adolescent with reading and writing difficulties becomes a successful real estate broker trading his ideas for profit by using tape-recorders and seductive secretaries taking down dictation rather than becoming a proof-reader for a large publishing house . . .

An adolescent with motoric and verbal hyperactivity becomes a "tummler" in the Borscht Belt rather than a professional bird-watcher (for explanations, check with your nearest Jewish friend).

But it is well to consider that indeed many youngsters with these troubles will probably be regarded in adulthood as "funny people,"—hazy, crazy, and/or lazy. In addition, we cannot be certain as to the type and extent of the emotional or psychological sequelae in adults who had these problems as obvious manifestations when they were children. There is no reason to surmise that there were any fewer patients with minimal cerebral dysfunction one generation ago than now. On the contrary, with improved prenatal, perinatal, and postnatal care and more effective methods of combatting illness via immunizations and medications and by overall better nutrition . . . we would expect *fewer* patients now than before. Yet, I am told, and this is a sticky statistic I know, that 10 to 15 percent of our children—who can see and hear adequately . . . whose IQs are within normal limits . . . of both sexes . . . of all ethnic groups—still have cognitive and/or behavioral problems, most probably based on minimal cerebral dysfunctioning with important secondary psychological sequelae. I prefer to look at the statistics in this way: that 10 to 15 percent of our children *can't* (at least originally, and this concept is almost crucial to my bias) learn and/or *can't* behave the way the other 85-90% do.

A brief digression now, if you will. At many of our information-giving lecture seminars with parents, older patients, teachers, and other involved professionals, there is a constantly recurring question theme: "Why do we seem to see more learning problems like dyslexia (we'll define it soon) than we did fifty years ago? Recurrent answers are:

We're more aware of dyslexia as a valid diagnosis . . .

Before, many were considered hazy, crazy, and/or lazy . . .

There's a greater emphasis now on schooling . . .

There's a greater emphasis now on reading . . .

There's a greater emphasis now on literary skills . . .

We are teaching reading the wrong way . . .

People have to go to school longer now . . .

More babies with perinatal troubles are being saved . . .

We're expecting more of children at an earlier age than we used to. And sometimes they are not developmentally ready for certain cognitive tasks . . .

Children do not have to make their toys as they used to. Toys are too prefabricated and so children have little chance for motor-perceptual development.

A good one I heard recently makes sense: With the increasing literacy rate, the percentage with inherent dyslexia will come to the fore. An interesting item was told to me recently by Sister Eileen-Marie Cronin of the Raskob Institute of the College of the Holy Names at Oakland, California: the Post Office Department indicates that in the middle 1800s, on the average, each person in the United States read only about four one-page letters per year.

In that situation it's hard to imagine dyslexia poking you in the shoulder and saying, "Here I am! Understand me! Cure me!"

The boy-girl ratio is pretty consistent. On many days at our learning disabilities clinic we see about 6-8 boys for every girl. The same ratio generally applies to the classes for the educationally handicapped. Why? I feel fairly certain that the reasons have to do with inherited genetic familial factors transmitted along male lines. However, I was once told (and not in jest, I believe) that the ratio favoring or rather *disfavoring* boys was because boys are generally heavier at birth. So? Well, it was explained like this: larger, heavier births ——→ more difficult deliveries ——→ more trouble at birth ——→ more subtle problems later in life.

I find this difficult to accept scientifically. Carefully controlled studies would have to be done. In addition, we'd have to take note of the fact that firstborns tend to be lighter in weight than their siblings. But are subsequent deliveries easier or more difficult? And how would we quantify easy or difficult? We do have systems for evaluating the neonatal condition. But how about measuring the difficulty or ease of the delivery itself? By number of hours of labor? By what one's mother-in-law claims? I do not pretend to have the answers. On the other hand, follow-up studies of premature children seem to bear out the fact, in part at least, that the younger and lighter the premature infant (especially the very small ones), the greater the chance for neurological impairment. One could write a book on the studies of premature children alone; there are differences of opinion.

This chance business is interestingly unnerving. Here comes a half digression and it has to do with how much information of the "chance type" we should give to parents. This is information which, in a sense, we're really not sure about in that it does not specifically relate to one patient . . . because we're talking about percentages in groups. If we can make a firm diagnosis of mongolism or certain chromosomal aberrations shortly after birth by relatively clear clinical evidence and laboratory testing . . . that's one thing. We can level with the patient's parents and tell them what our experience with these definitely diagnosed groups has been. But even in such groups—I believe—there is a continuum of possible cognitive and emotional achievement depending on:

how much pre-injury in how many body systems there is . . .

how much environmental love is given . . .

how much environmental enrichment is given.

Often I rely on and pass on to parents the old notion of "Expect the worst, but hope for the best."

But let us consider some groups which do not fit neatly in one or another diagnostic category. Like infants who do not begin to walk until two years of age. Or children who do not make simple sentences until four years of age. I think we'd all agree that each infant and child of such groups should benefit from *individualized* assessment and remediation. But what of groups of "normals?" What are the chances that some members of the "normal" group will or will not develop

> neurological damage (kind and extent?)
>
> cerebral palsy (kind and extent?)
>
> retardation (kind and extent?)

Once, at an interdisciplinary meeting, some professionals of a background other than mine advocated the advantages of their team's early testing of normals . . . at about 18 months of age ("normals" refers to infants whose developmental milestones are clinically OK). By their method, they could expect to identify those youngsters who were to have future neurological problems. Those professionals, ponderous with prodigious pride, put forth the statistics that in fully 90 percent of the ones tested (allow me to mention my hemi-homonym—i.e., in 90 percent of the *once-tested*) the prediction of future trouble or no trouble was correct—high correlation with tests administered . . . statistically significant . . . scientifically valid . . . etc., etc., etc.

But as the concept unfolded I became more and more unglued and unhinged and finally bolted. *What of the 10 percent of the normal group wherein the prediction was wrong?* A prediction which could riddle with anxiety the parents, the patient, and the involved professionals, *either way:*

> that an infant who was supposed to be OK wouldn't be . . .
> that an infant who was supposed to be NOT OK would be
> . . . And no one knows for sure until three or four years later in which 10 percent of the group the prediction was wrong.

I am not proposing the withholding of information. But I violently believe in nonviolent information giving! So in any new study of normal 18-month-old infants with the same tests and the same experimental design they can tell parents that in nine of ten cases their prediction will be correct; but in one of ten the prediction will be wrong either way.

As a parent I can do without this type of percentage-of-normal-group information, this type of solace, this type of peace of mind . . . so that I can keep my piece of mind.

At this point, one lady in the audience apprised us that as a result of one-shot testing some seven years ago, a presumptive diagnosis of retardation was made for her then 12-month-old baby. That youngster, now a third grader, had come home with three A's and two B's last week. I'm nervous about one-shot testing in general because one or more of the three C's which can constrict even civilization's progress might have been operating that day to make invalid that one test—colic, coryza, constipation. (Those of us who have been possessed, know.) Long-term observations—up to that point at which practical and realistic decisions have to be made—are preferable and beneficial to patient, parents, and professionals.

It was then, at that meeting that the other discipline jumped me: "Well, *Doctor* (with saturated sarcasm rather than sweeping sincerity), don't you ever want to know about future trouble? Don't you want to be properly prepared?" Sure I want to know, as a physician and a parent, but I don't want to worry about something that I really can't do much about because it hasn't happened yet. However, I do believe in school readiness testing, which I feel is appropriate and valuable at about four and a half years of age—in the months before kindergarten. Early diagnosis and prevention are concepts of great reason to me, but I feel that individual development and maturation should be given a chance, at least until the prekindergarten months. There are enough youngsters, especially boys, who fit into the group of delayed-maturers or late-bloomers* to suggest that later testing is advisable. Delayed maturation—and this is a very sticky diagnosis—can occur, I feel, up until ten or twelve years of age and is often difficult to distinguish from minimal cerebral dysfunction. Long-term observation (or foot-dragging and fence-walking, as some of my friends (?) have called it) often helps to distinguish the two, but not always. Testing too late or diagnosing school problems too late results in many deleterious sequelæ both cognitive and

---

*At this point in our chronicle I got a bit upset and I'd like to tell you about it. I sensed that the term "late-bloomer" was a good setup for a humorous aside like: "No relationship to the undergarment industry intended." But I was afraid it was too earthy and I might offend. Anyway, I thought I'd let you in on it.

emotional. But premature testing with its almost ever-present labeling has no uniform success either, and therefore I think that readiness assessment at about four and a half years is optimal. And even then please take readiness test results with grains of salt. Let's try to maintain a broad concept of what "within normal limits" is.

Vignette A

Our first-born son (I'll not mention his name for fear he'll want royalties) when he was five years old was asked, "You've been to the store . . . you go to the corner . . . it's raining . . . a bus comes along . . . a bus that goes directly to your home . . . what would you do?" Our scion never wavered: "I'd go back into the store . . . to the telephone." An inappropriate response! . . . Psychopathology? Cognitive malfunctioning? Boredom? A concerned teacher . . . A hurried call to a mother about to serve a match point . . . she double faults . . . A hurried call to a father about to mend a hurt joint . . . he somersaults . . . (Please note the rhyme scheme— it took me 20 minutes to figure it out.) A quickly arranged meeting among teacher, child, parents . . . "Why would you have done what you said you'd do given the above circumstances?" the little lad is asked. Notwithstanding the confusing syntactics of the question, his answer rings true and clear. "I'd do what you told me to do, Daddy: 'If it rains . . . always call for a taxi.'" (It has to do with an old family myth that a wet head might decrease intellectual functioning—perhaps the origin of the 1940s put-down epithet: "You drip!") We coughed a cough of relief. But to prepare for further testing situations, we are taking rainy-day bus rides at least three times per year. A desperate dilemma diagnosed!

Vignette B

Our third-born son (I'll not mention his name for fear he'll want royalties) was taking his four-and-a-half-year-old pre-kindergarten readiness test . . . was doing very well . . . knew the tactics that Miltiades used at Marathon . . . explained the deficiencies of $E=mc^2$ . . . commented on the derivation of Rembrandt's chiaroscuro. But then the fateful question: "When does Christmas come —in winter or summer?" The testor had already marked him as correct when the little lad blithely answered: "Summer!" He

*was doing so well until then! An inappropriate response! . . .
Psychopathology? Cognitive malfunctioning? Boredom? A concerned
testor . . . My Lawfully-Wedded, standing nearby, whispered
gently to the testor: "Rosenthal?" My Lawfully-Wedded
almost drew a Star-of-David next to the name "Rosenthal," but
I have cautioned her regarding the pitfalls of early labeling. The
testor looked at my Lawfully-Wedded and thought; "But you
look so Anglo-Saxonish." But then, with diction lessons, hair
bleaching, stretching exercises, and the plastic surgery procedure
of proboscis concavization . . . anything is possible . . . Mediterraneans
can be changed into Nordics?*

*Well, it finally turned out that as a traveling family and because
Christmas isn't really our holiday, we try to get away at
that time as often as we can. And so the Christmases that our
third son knew in his second, third, and fourth years were spent
in Acapulco, Oahu, and Kona with all of the summery sights,
sounds, aromas, tastes, and touches thereunto appertaining. And
so what might have been the first recorded case of SISU (Specific
Isolated Season Unknowingness) turned out to be CSIBOT (Cognitive
Seasonal Interchange Because of Travel). A profound puzzle
pierced!*

Vignette C

*An IQ testing situation. An adolescent boy—bright, alert, verbal.
Doing quite well until one of the questions came. "How many
ears do you have?" Without blinking an eye . . . the answer came:
"Fifteen!" An inappropriate response! . . . Psychopathology?
Cognitive malfunctioning? Boredom? A concerned testor . . .
But Father Slade Crawford is sensitive to his environment and
is not bound rigidly by "wrong" answers. He noted that the
young man had a Spanish surname. He noted that the young
man was fifteen years old. Father Crawford diagnosed not Hazy,
Crazy, and/or Lazy but rather PHONEMICITIS—the inflammation
of the young man's phonemic or sound systems, wherein,
in a bilingual speaker, one sound system (Spanish) might rub off
on the other (English) at times, so that this young, bright, verbal,
bilingual boy had heard: "How many years do you have?" Which
is a clear word-by-word translation from the Spanish idiom
"Cuantos años tiene Usted?" And he had answered quite appropriately:
"Fifteen!" An enormous enigma explained!*

Vignette D

An IQ testing situation. A ten-year-old boy—bright, alert, verbal. Doing quite well until one of the questions came: "If you go to the store to buy a loaf of bread and there aren't any left, what would you do?" Without a second thought the answer came: "I'd go home and we'd bake some." Right answer? Wrong answer? Partially right answer? Partially wrong answer? How's an IQologist to grade? INFORMATIONAL BULLETIN: It just so happens that in that family they—men and women, boys and girls—just love to bake bread! A refractory riddle resolved!

Well, we certainly have wandered a bit since the definition of minimal cerebral or brain dysfunction was given earlier in this chapter. My second change to the definition was to add the word "and" between "learning" and "or behavior." What I mean to stress is that cognitive (thinking, academic, learning) problems and behavioral problems are not mutually exclusive. They may indeed co-exist. It is also possible that cognitive problems might cause behavioral problems. That is, a youngster who can see and hear and whose general IQ is well within normal limits and who is not primarily emotionally disturbed *still* may do poorly in academic areas which will be discussed later, for reasons he or she is not aware of. In great part because the youngster doesn't understand why he or she can't learn as the others do, feelings of diminished self-worth grow—and often lead to aggressive, antisocial behavior. Moreover, behavioral problems whether of organic or psychogenic causes can cause academic problems.

For example, an organically hyperactive-distractable youngster can't sit still long enough or is so diverted from the task at hand by irrelevant stimuli that he has great difficulty in processing information as his peers do. Or a youngster who is emotionally distressed for personal or family reasons can't learn well when his thoughts and worries are elsewhere.

I have a bias—not a prejudice—which I'd like to touch on now. I do feel, after working with 1100 patients, their families, their schools, and their peers in the learning disabilities clinic, that I can say this: most of the cognitive and/or behavioral problems they have are primarily based on biochemical, organic, neurological, electrophysiological, and physical factors—albeit in subtle ways—as stated above in the definition of minimal brain dysfunction. However, there seems to be little doubt that in just about all of our patients with learning and/or behavioral problems there are almost immediate emotional upsets, varying in degree, of a secondary nature. They are there! Yet even when they are of overwhelming significance they are secondary and not primary, I feel. They are effects not causes, and it is important to distinguish them. These physical and emotional factors become progressively and confusingly intertwined, especially as our patients get older. We'll get into this more, later on.

You know, it's getting to be a pretty long chapter . . . so why don't we take a break. A salami and Swiss cheese sandwich? Or pay some attention to your patiently waiting companion. Or, for those who simply cannot put the book down, on to the next chapter.

Developing
definitions
daguerreotypishly

Several other points should be made regarding the definition of minimal brain dysfunction. First of all, I'm talking about general intelligence that's near average, average, or above average. Intelligence is quite tough to explain, let alone define. Basic psychology texts imply that it has to do with qualities which allow for an individual's successful adjustment to his environment—and, of course, we could discuss that for a few months. And what's the meaning of "an individual," "successful," and "environment?" Also, places and times are relative because they change. Some five thousand years ago intelligence, defined as successful adaptation to one's surroundings, could have been seen differently from the way it is today. . . . (This is one of my favorite spiels. I'll go into it later.)

. . . In 3550 BC intelligence had to do with bow and arrow talents in a hunting society—both design and marksmanship (markswomanship too?) aspects taken into account. An MGA (Master of Game Archery) might have been given at that time by Nomad State College. Courses, which were mostly lab, had to be taken at several different and widely spread campuses, of course.

. . . In 2562 BC, a BAA (Bachelor of Agrarian Arts) might have been given by the Antiochus Agricultural Academy for proficiency in seed-planting. Angle of fling as well as strength counted in the final grading.

. . . In 1235 BC Phonicia Polytech might have given a PhD in the seafaring arts—both navigational and knot-tying talents were requisite.

There were few paper-and-pencil success tasks then as equivalents of intelligence. There were few colleges and fewer graduate schools, and certainly the foreign language requirement was not enforced—especially before the building of the Tower of Babel.

To get back to the definition of intelligence, I know people who would say there is a materialistic, acquisitive aspect to its meaning and that it has to do with . . . yes . . . with adjusting well to the environment. But also with getting the most out of the environment . . . while putting in the least . . . and causing the fewest waves. (This isn't my idea of course, just that of some people I know.)

So intelligence is like: manipulativeness of the mind—not necessarily moralistic. Craftiness of the consciousness—not necesarily with conscience. Shrewdness of the senses—not necessarily with chivalry. (This isn't my idea of course, just that of some people I know.)

Moreover, there's increasing evidence that there are several types of intelligence, generally divided into verbal and performance abilities. Here we get into some fascinating aspects of brain (cortical) localization of certain functions. It appears that the left side of the brain has to do with verbal and language abilities while the right side is associated with spatial and geometric talents. I'm sure we've all met, known, and enviously despised those unbelievably accomplished ones . . .

> handsome and rich—and they haven't even used the inheritance money yet . . .
>
> who hit smashing backhands on the tennis court . . .
>
> who talk with ease and extemporaneously about existential philosophy . . .
>
> who possess that slick dash to cause discomfiture in the maitre d'hotel of you-know-where.

To put it succinctly, both sides of their heads are working well and together. Alas, however, for me, being a verbalist (superfluously my friends? would say) and language-oriented, my left brain by extension (pushiness?) is causing my left ear to sit further off my head. I am also balder over my left scalp, probably because of increased tension there. On the other hand, the world of the woodshop has remained an exotic mystery to me all these years. How my father-in-law could design and make functional (and beautiful) tables, chairs, and lamps is still a universal unknown for me. And so I would guess that were a flashlight to be placed to the right of my head, it probably would shine directly through like the searching September spotlights announcing the new auto models. I get splinters by just looking at redwood, but

I think that's another problem. Let the Freudians make of it what they will.

To be clinical for a moment, we have as one of our patients a delightful, bright, young lad who has a specific reading disability (dyslexia) showing itself more as a word-perception problem than a sound-symbol difficulty. His father is a bright, urbane, and erudite mathematics professor who would much rather teach algebra than geometry—because to this day, to his despair, he has trouble forming geometric figures on the blackboard. At times his students even laugh at him. He does get embarrassed. Could there be some sort of inherited-genetic pattern here relating to the inability to work well with forms—either as words on a page or as figures on a blackboard? There is evidence for this.

Is it possible, genetically, to be really smart in the left brain but not so smart in the right brain? And to be so smart in the left brain that through the years you've learned to "language yourself" around the right-brain jobs that come up? And vice versa? We all know people who can't seem to put it nicely together in words, either orally or on paper—but who can, with facility, draw it or make it to show you what they mean.

Are we touching here on some causes of the wide divergences we often see in the language and spatial capacities of patients with minimal brain dysfunction? Interestingly, there seems to be some evidence, albeit in need of verification, that right- and left-brained people look to different sides when asked questions. It appears that right-brained folks tend to look to the left and left-brained folks to the right while they're thinking about their answers. We'd have to develop a rigorous scientific design to test these preliminary findings—a design with questions which would require verbal or relational-spatial cerebral wheel-spinning to get the answers. Research is now being done with electroencephalographic alpha waves to determine which side of the brain is turned on with which cognitive tasks, either language or spatial. Some interesting correlations might be found between the eye and the alpha wave studies. At any rate, a penetrating new criterion has finally appeared on l'amour's horizon: one may now choose a close friend or soulmate via the standard of brain-sidedness—the latter creating a selection triumvirate of the former duo, individual voluptuousness and family wealth. Match-computers and marriage-brokers, attention and beware! Can a left-brained girl and a right-brained boy really survive in our society? And vice versa? Can they possibly be Scrabble partners? Is the final analysis of life's psychodrama to be found in the verbal charade? Does this offer a neurophysiologic basis for the popular but cruel insult—"half-brain?"

We should touch for a moment on the concept of the idiot-savant because it might well relate to the ultimate personification of the full right-left brain dichotomy. Through history, idiot-savants are those who, while incomparably inept in some areas, are tremendously talented in others. In my own experience—as an extension of the above concept: in grade school there was Abie (pseudonym) who memorized infinite baseballian minutiæ— hitting averages, runs batted in, home runs, bases stolen by lefties and righties on and off their birthdays—of some 500 athletes. But to throw a baseball anywhere within the 180° arc just in front was for him an impossible accomplishment. In high school, Georgie (pseudonym) had great trouble with academic subjects. He was bouncy and hyperactive (to be defined) but was a great, great piano player . . . although he never had a lesson and couldn't read a note. He did it all by ear.

And so it would appear that there is something wrong with the notion that the head is totally good *or* totally bad, totally right *or* totally wrong, totally on *or* totally off, totally up *or* totally down. Rather, some abilities and talents might be functioning well and others not. My bias is that OK or not OK functioning is neurophysiologically and not psychologically based. But clearly in all these examples, secondary, florid emotional problems almost immediately come into play when such divergent thinkings and behaviors occur in the head of the same person . . . and the world doesn't understand why.

In our definition of minimal brain dysfunction we are talking about general intelligence being OK. I'm talking about a little lad of eleven who is alert, bright, verbally sharp—and yet who can't read past the second-grade level. He can see and hear. He is not primarily emotionally disturbed and has had an adequate educational experience. And he has tried! Oh, how he has tried to learn to read! Is he stupid, dumb, retarded, MR, and/or nuts? He could and did: manage to con the kids to con the teacher to create Wednesday PM's as "liberated gum-chewing afternoons" (a nonnegotiable demand). And then he bought gum for 1¢ apiece on Tuesday PM's . . . and sold it on Wednesday PM's . . . to kids who forgot to bring gum . . . but for 2¢ apiece. That's 100% profit! He created the whole enterprise: first the need, then the delivery. He caught frogs in the suburbs and sold them to the city slickers. His mind was masterfully manipulative as long as you didn't ask him to read or spell. He had great trouble in deciphering graphic symbols so that they made sense to him. He also had difficulty in putting his thoughts into appropriate written form. My counseling sessions with him were mostly of an informative nature:

> explaining what he *wasn't*—dumb, nuts, and/or goofing off . . .

> explaining what he *was*—a youngster with dyslexia and dysgraphia (you'll just have to read on to find out what these are) . . .

I couldn't help being pleased with—and indeed I reinforced—his commercial ventures. My thinking was that nonacademic success might well intergeneralize with academic achievement, both resulting in growth of self-esteem and motivation.

But, as in all dramatic two-hour movies, after the scenario had run about 1¼ hours his mother called frantically. He had been expelled from school . . . business had been so good . . . he decided to expand . . . into the protection racket. I quickly recounseled him and explained the limits of acceptable entrepreneurism in our society. He was contrite, returned the money, and went back into the gum business.

Referring back to our definition of minimal brain dysfunction, we're talking about learning and/or behavioral disabilities ranging from mild to severe. There is a teasing relativity in the continuum from mild to severe, based not only on the nature and extent of the disorder but also on time, place, age, achievement emphasis, and ease of problem concealment.

An example of a mild problem: Mr. Jones is 45 years old and can read but a few words. Realizing this, with his generally good intelligence, he doesn't try to read and he doesn't become frustrated. He reasoned well, many years ago, that a skill involving literary talents was not for him. He was not put down by teachers, parents, siblings, friends, parents of friends, grandparents, or his wife—even though they didn't really understand why this seemingly bright fellow had trouble with reading, spelling, and writing. He didn't make waves in the classroom or in society and so he left school at the minimum legal age, having caused very little friction. Because he was facile with his hands and mechanically minded, he became an auto mechanic—a good one, a successful one, a contented one. He's happily married, attends church regularly, and plays ball with his children (but doesn't help them with their homework). He has some trouble with menus when dining out but has memorized "New York Steak" almost as a pictograph; luckily, he likes it very much.

Mr. Jones is an example of a mind problem. His oldest son, now eight years of age, is starting to have some trouble in reading at school. The teachers are getting concerned and are indicating to the parents that something should be done. But that's another problem. Or is it?

An example of a severe problem: Edward Jr. is a bright little lad of five and a half. He was born in late November and just got into kindergarten before the legal cutoff date. His parents were happy about this because they thought that with all Edward Jr. had going for him, why start school a whole year later just because it had almost taken a few weeks too long for passion to overwhelm Edward Sr.? Edward Jr. is finishing his kindergarten year in a sophisticated suburban setting where it is common knowledge that there is a direct relationship between academic achievement (the earlier the better of course) and eventual socio-economic status—that is, the best business positions (including life insurance and retirement benefits!) . . . the best residential locations (including low down-payments and ease-of-freeway-access benefits!) . . . and the best wives (including . . . including . . . well, you know, all sorts of benefits!). Anyway, in early May it became manifest that Edward Jr. didn't know all his letters by name or sound; and when he should have been reading at .9K he was reading at only .3K; and he had some difficulty in paying attention; and one substitute teacher even said of him: "Possibly hyperactive."

Between his parents there are three degrees (academically speaking) which almost jumped five degrees (feverishly speaking) when it was suggested that—because of Edward Jr.'s immaturity—retention in kindergarten might be a good idea. There was a family crisis, reaching to the venerated halls of one of the great Eastern Universities where one of the grandparents was teaching. This crisis included:

trans-USA telephone calls . . .

psychological examinations . . .

neurological examinations . . .

psychiatric examinations . . .

developmental examinations . . .

speech and language examinations . . .

motor-perceptual examinations . . .

eye training examinations . . .

and counseling, discussions, meetings, more telephone calls . . . etc., etc., etc.

With controversy causing confusion: some professionals spoke in terms of "psychological blocks" which caused the school problems; other specialists indicated "brain damage" as the basis for the learning blocks.

Tutors, at first of the parental variety, were tried. Father, tired after his day, attempted to work with son, tired after his day, at 7:30 PM. Inevitable tensions led to strains, outbursts, recriminations, tears. What to do? Nonparental tutors? Summer school? Private school? Special training? Educationally handicapped classes? Full-time or part-time? Family counseling? Individual psychotherapy? With so many choices offered, it reminds me of an old notion in the philosophy of the therapeutic arts. If there are many treatment possibilities for one clinical problem, then probably no single one of them has been consistently found to be really successful. For example, generally speaking, there is a treatment of choice for a streptococcal sore throat, appendicitis, or a fractured radius. But not so for the problems of Edward Jr. For a five-and-a-half-year-old, he has big, big troubles. And so do his involved kinfolk and professionals.

On the other hand, another father of another kindergartener with a similar difficulty—I remember this father quite well because he was a large man with big hands and an open, reddish, sensitive face—once said to me poignantly: "Doc, can you really flunk sandbox?"

Pertaining to our definition, my feeling is that most of the problems we are talking about—subtle variations from whatever "normal" is in thinking and/or behavior—are based on minimal dysfunctions of the cerebrum (brain). This is not to deny (in fact it is important to stress and restress) that secondary, severe emotional complications can and do occur and that, especially in older patients, it is often difficult but vital to distinguish organic from psychogenic and primary from secondary.

Back to our definition again, we are concerned with:

- *Perception*—not vision but rather *how* the brain interprets what we see and sense.

- *Conceptualization*—the ability to think abstractly and not only concretely: two different talents, the disabilities for the former and the abilities for the latter possibly existing side by side in the same brain . . . and vice versa.

- *Language*—not speech (which is more motoric a function) but the decoding, storage, and encoding of the underlying functions of language as cognitive skills.

- *Memory*—not just as one faculty but at least as differences in short-term and long-term memory.

- *Control of attention*—the ability, neurophysiologically, to attend to relevant stimuli and to successfully sidetrack irrelevant stimuli.

- *Control of impulse*—the ability to count to ten and to make a judgment based more on reason than on emotion. Or the ability to react rationally on the basis of reason . . . or to react emotionally on the basis of reason . . . but not to react emotionally on the basis of emotion. That is, the opposite of the "short-fused kid."

- *Control of motor function*—the ability to get one's body and parts of one's body to do what one's brain wants to do. As well as getting one's body and parts of one's body *not* to do what one's brain *doesn't* want to do.

Before we go on to the next chapter, here is a thought about prematurity and its scholastic aftermaths—but chronologically rather than developmentally speaking. I have often thought upon the clear differences between little girl and boy kindergarteners. Little girls tend to be verbal, alert, classroom-oriented, paper-and-pencil-task-oriented, and usually ready. Little boys tend to be spatial, ingenuous, playground-oriented, slide-and-swing-task-oriented, and often not ready. Developmentally they are different. And by school standards girls generally are readier, most will agree—despite the argument that it is the matriarchy of the early grades which favors the girls.

But chronologically, what about the poor little guy who *in addition* was born in October or November and just got into kindergarten before the cutoff date? Many parents, wisened by hard experience, in appropriate situations will start their boys one year later. Repeating kindergarten is noted in the cumulative folder; starting a year later is . . . well, no one will ever know.

But then what of the premature child—girl or boy, but especially the boy—whose mother delivered after 32 to 36 weeks' gestation instead of the full term of 40 weeks, and who weighed but 3½ to 4½ pounds at birth, and who also was born in October or November?

Chronologically this prematurely born baby boy will, nonetheless, start school before his fifth birthday like all the other children. But is he really *like* all the other children? He should have been in his mother's womb, nature tells us, from four to eight weeks longer to attain his full development. And we're not really talking here about the developmental aspects of prematurity. Do they indeed catch up? When? My emphasis is that if the pregnancy had gone to term, that baby boy would have been born in December or January . . . not as a premature infant . . . and would have started kindergarten a whole year later . . . probably a boon, especially for a boy. The moral:

> Think sweetly of your sweetheart
> Around St. Valentine's Day
> But avoid lusty thoughts . . .
> Especially if there's a family history of prematurity.

An interesting if unnerving new criterion in family planning . . .

Motor-Perceptual Problems

"He who knows not history must relive it . . ." *

. . . And even if he does know it he still seems to have to relive it— most of the time, anyway **

This chapter relates part of the natural history of minimal cerebral dysfunctions—how they came to be known to us—so that we can believe and appreciate that they exist . . . in their many disguised forms . . . and that we might not have to fight the battle to prove their existence . . . again.

I often stress, when in pedagogic situations, that knowledge of *time* and *place* is necessary before one can really get to the substance of a topic:

> . . . the Aztecs of Mexico fought the Spaniards in the early 1500s . . .
>
> . . . the Vikings plundered Europe from the 9th to the 11th century . . .
>
> . . . the Mongols swept from Asia in the early 13th century.

But history is not just temporal and geographic. When spiced with salty and sultry sundries, it is alive, attractive—even alluring.

---

*I'm pretty sure George Santayana said it, but I'm not sure where or when.
**I said it.

Historical Vignette A

Time: *1066 AD*

Place: *Hastings, England*

Narrative: *William the Conqueror and his Normans defeat the English under Harold.*

Sundries: *That the English were tired from fighting other Norsemen shortly before Hastings and that William won by a feigned retreat is interesting. But history comes alive when Creasy in his* Fifteen Decisive Battles *(Everyman's Library, J. M. Dent & Sons, Ltd., 1851) describes this post-battle pathetic poignancy: from the mass of slaughtered bodies, the English King could not be recognized until his mistress Edith, called "the fair" and the "swan-necked," was sent for. Her eyes of love were more sensitive than those of the others and she found her Harold among the dead.*

Historical Vignette B

Time: *The winter of 1812-1813 AD*

Place: *Russia*

Narrative: *The retreat from Moscow of Napoleon's once grand Grand Armée, formerly 500,000 strong, turns into a nightmare for the French. Fewer than 100,000 manage to return to the borders of their homeland. The Emperor is sent to his Elba exile.*

Sundries: *Visions of splendid French Cavalry squadrons and proud infantry battalions withering in disarray are images I have often conjured up. And, yes, I can see and sense them now—the major causes of defeat, nay, the debacle: the Russian Winter (no adjective can really describe it) . . . and hunger . . . and the fierce Cossacks . . . and the love for Mother Russia by her people . . . and . . . oh, yes, Rickettsia Prowazeki, Salmonella sp., and Shigella sp.! (Oh, oh!! Rosenthal's been writing in the hot sun again!!)*

Well, actually, that's kind of true. I mean the part about writing this section in the hot sun. To balance the Russian winter, so to speak. But my Cognitive Marbles haven't really all rolled out yet. In a fact-filled but still very funny (at least in parts, at least to me) book by Hans Zinsser, titled *Rats, Lice and History*, Little, Brown and Co., 1935, this great bacteriologist emphasizes

60

that Napoleon was whipped less by Cossacks and the Russian winter and more by typhus and dysentery—at least as noted in differences in actual casualties caused by the latter and the former. His thesis, which is somewhat staggering in relation to the romanticized versions we have of military campaigns, is that it was really not so much.

Horatius finally alone holding off Rome's enemies at the bridge . . .

the treachery that doomed the chivalrous Roland . . .

the ill-fated Light Brigade's charge at Balaklava . . .

But rather that in the course of history the outcomes of battles and wars have been determined less by strategy and more by germs, germs, germs! And that Napoleon should have listened less to his artillery and attack officers and more to his sanitation and medical advisors. Mais, c'est la guerre; c'est la vie.

I was thinking how much fun it might be to zip up the time-place factors in the historical sciences. For example, suppose Sir Isaac Newton had been allergic to apples and was cautioned by his physician never to think, much less dally, under those fruit trees. The falling apple would never have hit the great physicist in the head and the realization of the theory of gravity might have been decades away. Could a falling kumquat have had the same impact on Newton's thinking? (I simply adore double entendres, don't you?)

How come Euclid was so cornered with angles and curves? (Let the Freudians make of it what they will.)

If the Tower of Pisa weren't leaning, how long might it have taken for Galileo to develop the laws of falling bodies?

Weight-volume water displacement proofs might never have come about if Archimedes had preferred showers to baths.

Medico-Historical Vignette C

Act I

Time: *1831*

Place: *Paris, France*

Narrative: *A man had lost his power of "speech." This was his only problem: he could not talk. He expressed himself intelligently via signs and seemed mentally normal from other points of view. He was hospitalized at the Bicêtre, an insane asylum.*

Act II

Time: *1861—thirty years later (obviously)*

Place: *Paris, France*

Narrative: *The above-mentioned patient with the "speech" problem remained at the Bicêtre for thirty years after which time he developed a gangrenous infection. He came under the care of a French surgeon, Paul Broca. Despite Broca's efforts the patient died. But before his patient's death, Broca, via extensive examination, was sure that:*

> *it was not a matter of low intelligence which hindered speech . . .*
>
> *the muscles of the larynx (voice box) were in order . . .*
>
> *the muscles that had to do with articulation in speech were in order . . .*
>
> *there was no other peripheral paralysis that could account for the problem.*

As described in Boring's History of Experimental Psychology *(Appleton-Century-Crofts, Inc., 1929), Broca performed an autopsy and discovered nothing anatomically damaged—except a lesion in the third frontal convolution of the left cerebral (cortex) hemisphere.*

Sundries: *Could it have been (and could it also now be) that a definitive lesion, damage, insult, or hurt (whatever the cause: bruise, blood clot, infection, tumor, genetically determined dysfunction) to a specific part of the brain might result in a specific loss of function? As was the case with Broca's patient? . . . And that the man really wasn't "insane." That is, in the insane sense of insane. And that he had a problem in language processing on a central cognitive basis rather than a speech problem on a peripheral-motor basis. And . . . now, here we go, here we go . . . and that maybe, just maybe (get the dramatic buildup now) . . . certain specific parts of the brain might control certain specific bodily functions . . . motoric, cognitive, and behavioral (that is, localization of function) . . . and that it might just be possible . . . under certain conditions . . . to debilitate, disable, and even destroy certain functions . . . while leaving the others intact in our complicated cerebral computers . . . so that the brain isn't neces-*

sarily totally good or totally bad . . . so that the brain isn't neces-
sarily OK or not OK . . . so that the brain isn't necessarily com-
pletely with it or not with it . . . but that rather, at times it's
possible to note divergences and discrepancies in its total func-
tioning . . . a notion which I hope I have alluded to in the first
six chapters . . . at first somewhat surreptitiously . . . and now
saliently and strikingly . . . and finally, I hope, successfully . . .

At this point I should mention the dogma struggle between the *equipotentialists* and the *multipotentialists* with relation to brain (cortical, cerebral) functioning—which is pretty heady stuff, I might add. The *equipotentialists* stress that much brain tissue is, at least originally, undifferentiated enough so that if an insult occurs in one sector other sectors assume functional responsibility for the damaged part. The *multipotentialists* favor the concept of relatively discrete localization of function for specific areas of the brain. This is clearly a simplified statement of two points of view for which there are many both positive and contradictory data, and also many subtheories and connecting theories. As with most of life's dilemmas, the truth (if we can ever finally define that artful dodger) lies probably somewhere, but not necessarily always in the same spot, between the two. For example, we do know that the earlier in age a definite lesion occurs, the greater the chance to recoup lost function. Maturational-developmental processes probably play roles, especially in young patients. The maturation of the brain is a subject of tantalizing interest in itself—not only from the points of view of how and where in the brain it occurs, but also *when.* That is to say, when is maturation complete? Ever? Just because a six-year-old's head circumference approaches that of an adult, does it follow that head growth and brain development have pretty much finished by that time? Probably not. Recent information indicates that the process of myelinization or the sheathing of nerve fibers (probably a maturational attribute) might well continue up to (and through?) adolescence.

Time out for a moment of Scientifico-Fantasy: Wouldn't it be a boon to knowledge if we could, in some way, make positive correlations between the neurophysiological maturational stages of myelinization and the clinical developmental stages of Jean Piaget? For example, does Piaget's Formal Reasoning Stage start at about 11 to 13 years of age because of neuro-anatomico-physiological preparedness? And just think of the delightfully provocative ethnic and cultural implications! Did the biblical patriarchs anticipate Piaget by several thousands of years? Why else then is that quintessence of intertwining abstract mentation—the Bar Mitzvah—set for age 13?

We haven't even discussed the nutritional aspects of maturation, both prenatal and postnatal. Much information is becoming available from human studies and from animal experiments. It would take tomes and tomes to go through these studies adequately. Certainly nutrition—and malnutrition—play decisive roles in the developing nervous system.

With respect to the dogma struggle mentioned above, my bias is toward *multipotentialism*. It appeals to my inherent love (need? Can we separate the two at times?) for geographic localization and differentiation—both cartographic and cortical. Something happens to me when I see diminutive Liechtenstein wedged between Austria and Switzerland on a map. And I know that the Liechtensteiners have their own individuality in areas that really make a difference: as the last remnant of the Holy Roman Empire . . . with beautifully engraved postage stamps . . . and relatively low taxes. I get similar sensations from Monaco, San Marino, and Andorra. (Let the Freudians make of it what they will.) Other reasons for my support of *multipotentialism* are:

- it seems to be scientifically truer . . .
- it better supports the concept of subtle cognitive and behavioral changes based on minimal brain dysfunctioning . . .
- I use it as one of my "spiels" in the office.

Our natural history of the minimal brain dysfunctions—some clinical manifestations of which are the learning disabilities, cognitive and/or behavioral—comes to us from many sources. I will touch on three. If we can learn from this history, we might *not* have to relive it. The three sources are:

- information from patients who suffered definitive brain damage in war
- information from patients with definitive brain damage, obtained during neurosurgical procedures
- information from patients with definitive brain damage as a result of strokes (cerebro-vascular accidents)

Thousands of articles and books have been written about such damage but the terminologies—even intraprofessionally, much less interprofessionally—are not completely clear and standardized.

I'll try not to sacrifice honest doubt and theory for the sake of neat packaging and "final truths."

In war, people may suffer wounds in various locations ranging in severity from mild insults to those causing deafness, blindness, retardation, paralysis, epilepsy, or even death. Kurt Goldstein was a physician with the German army in World War I. He studied some 2000 soldier-patients longitudinally over a period of ten years. These patients had suffered definitive trauma to the head—that is, gunshot wounds. Goldstein described his findings in *After-Effects of Brain Injuries in War* (Grune and Stratton, 1942). Among his conclusions were these:

- Not all individuals with gunshot wounds to the general area of the head were affected in the same way.
- The varieties of impairment corresponded relatively well with the brain areas which were damaged.
- Traumatic dementia was different from senile dementia.
- Not all of a person's faculties (cognitive and behavioral abilities) had suffered. (I feel this is crucial.)

In other words it was *not*, with relation to brain damage, a matter of

Yes or No in the entire brain . . .

100% or 0% in the entire brain . . .

All OK or all not-OK in the entire brain . . .

but rather that some talents were damaged while others were maintained. In reading Goldstein's book, I was overwhelmed with admiration for this man who showed insightful expertise in neurology, neurophysiology, and psychology as well as those grand virtues of patience and humanity. Permit me to extract parts of an illustrative case history. A 34-year-old man had suffered a left-brain wound: a projectile had entered through the left eye and had come out behind the left ear. After the wound healed, neurologically and communicatively he was all right except that his speech was practically devoid of nouns, adjectives, auxiliary verbs, and especially the names of concrete objects. Circumlocutions helped him express his ideas. He had severe *amnesic aphasia*. Efforts to build up new associations between objects and words by repetition failed. Goldstein concluded that the problem was one of impairment "of the abstract attitude." Naming objects generally belongs to this "abstract attitude." When speaking of "table," for example, usually one does not mean a special table, but table in general. For a person who has malfunctioning of the "abstract attitude," it is difficult to build associations between words and objects not concretely experienced. Goldstein suggested that this situation was similar to that of a person learning a foreign vocabulary he did not understand.

Wilder Penfield, a brilliant neurosurgeon from Montreal, has used mild electrical stimulation of the cortex during neurosurgical procedures to help gather information pertaining to localization of function (*Epilepsy and Cerebral Localization*—Charles C Thomas, 1941). Yet he stresses that the cerebral cortex is not a keyboard; rather, it possesses many different neural circuits. Functional localization exists not in "centers" or "points" in the cortex, but in arcs and patterns that extend into various regions of the brain. And so Penfield suggests that if the left thumb moves as a result of cortical stimulation at one point we can conclude, not that thumb movement is represented there only, but that a *part* of the neural connections involved in thumb movement is located at that point. When certain parts of his brain were stimulated, one of Penfield's patients reported many diverse but discrete feelings and movements: "Sensation in index finger and thumb, also arm; no movement." "Sensation in right shoulder and side of face." "Twitching of the right side of face, mouth drawn downward and slight vocalization."

Penfield describes another patient with seizures of a psychical nature. During surgery, stimulation of a cortical area near a scar of an old injury caused *behavioral* symptoms which included the emotional state usually preceding the psychical attacks as well as the attack itself, which included weeping, grinding of teeth, and attempts at clutching his own neck.

A great deal of fascinating information has come from the clinical neuropsychologist/research neurophysiologist partnership. The bibliography could easily number in the thousands but this was not meant to be such a book. Most of the information I am about to relate comes from *Brain Mechanisms Underlying Speech and Language*, edited by Millikan and Darley (Grune and Stratton, 1967). At this time it would be well to show a side-view of the brain indicating major areas (see Figure 2). The following is an overview only, with as many reservations as positive statements, and so I'll attempt to use as many subjunctives, if clauses, circumlocutions, and conditionals as possible to prevent future critics from pinning me down.

Generally, damage to the left and right parietal areas causes praxis or planning disorders, but in different ways. Ideomotor

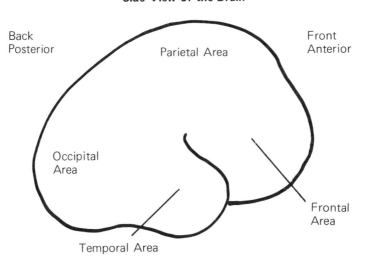

Figure 2

Side View of the Brain

Back
Posterior

Parietal Area

Front
Anterior

Occipital
Area

Frontal
Area

Temporal Area

and ideational apraxia seem to be always associated with left-hemisphere (left-brain) lesions (left brain = verbal, language functions). On the other hand, visuo-constructive disorders and dyspraxia for dressing (the Freudians could *really* dress this one up) occur with right-hemisphere (right-brain) lesions (right brain = spatial, geometric, relational functions). A fascinating problem is seen in certain patients with spatial problems involving disturbances in topographical concepts and memory, seemingly due to right-side lesions. This knowledge now enables me to make a phenomenal diagnosis in retrospect.

Vignette

It was 1952 . . . a hard time for the US Army of Occupation in Germany . . . I was allowed to bring over only one of my personal vehicles. When I saw St. Mark's Square in Venice, there was at least 20 feet between tourists . . . now there are at least 20 tourists per square foot, not counting the pigeons. I was a young, not-bald-yet, dashing ~~cavalry~~ (sorry, I almost galloped away with myself) medical officer. Times were tough . . . A brother officer had developed a sophisticated technique to get him through practical map-terrain exercises. (We were dumped in the German countryside . . . with only a map and our wits . . . and we had to get back to the base . . . with all haste before dark—or else no food!) Major

67

X invariably managed to beat us all back each time. The day before my discharge, he told me his secret . . . he just couldn't dig his maps so he used his wits. Which was to find the first German taxi . . . and for 10 marks he was soon friends with a Martini. Diagnosis: Right-Sided Parietal Dystopographia and Dysmapia! Scientifico-Fantasy: I am told that this major had almost reached Berlin with unprecedented military élan in the closing days of World War II, when a horrified Supreme Command hastily informed him that it had been his unit's mission to secure the approaches to Naples.

Three different types of mathematical difficulties (dyscalculia) are noted in parietal lesions:

- *Spatial dyscalculia:* operational difficulty because of faulty placing of figures or neglect of part of the figures, usually due to right-side problems.
- *Figure alexia:* reading troubles pertaining to the figures or numbers, usually due to left-side problems.
- *Anarithmetia:* loss of ability to carry out arithmetical operations, usually due to left-side but sometimes to right-side problems.

A Mathematical Problem by any other name is still a Mathematical Problem. But there seem to be different types of mathematical problems depending on which sub-operation is interfered with, and interesting and significant correlations are being uncovered with relation to anatomical localizations and specific functional problems.

The dyslexia and dysgraphia of right-side lesions are not the same as those of left-side lesions. In left-side lesions the problems relate more to faulty comprehension or transcription of graphic codes; in right-side lesions the reading and writing difficulties are due more to perceptual problems in the spatial arrangements of letters, words, and sentences. Spatial dyslexia occurs with occipital as well as parietal lesions. That two types of dyslexia might exist—each based on a different functional-anatomical etiology from a neurophysiological point of view—is impressive enough. But when one considers the *clinical* work of Elena Boder, a pediatric neurologist from Los Angeles who also delineates at least two types of dyslexia—one based on sound-symbol difficulties and the other due to Gestalt-spatial problems—the possible relationship between the two types of study become little short of fascinating. We'll get into more of this later on.

Certain types of callosal syndromes (disconnections between the brain hemispheres) can occur either with lesions or after required neurosurgery and lead to the preservation of certain task abilities despite the loss of others. These vary:

- Alexia may occur without agraphia
- Writing with one hand may be linguistically correct while writing with the other is aphasic
- The ability to name objects (but not colors) may be preserved
- Even the ability to name arabic (but not roman) numerals may be preserved

I see this last concept as stupefying. Two different localizations for two different math systems?

I haven't even discussed the different types of aphasia. I haven't mentioned the differences in long-term and short-term memory and how, with certain types of trauma, one may be compromised and the other maintained. In bilingual stroke patients, the neurophysiological and psychological aspects of which language returns first have been studied. There seem to be real differences and the speculations are provocative. The brain damage to a stroke patient varies, in part, depending on what blood vessel is blocked or thrombosed. The area of the brain with the resultant decreased blood supply is infarcted or functionally interfered with. Recovery depends on several factors.

As our history goes on, we should not forget the splendid work of Dr. Samuel T. Orton, who, in 1928, used the term *strephosymbolia* (from the Greek, meaning twisted symbols) to describe a group of children with specific reading disabilities.

And now we come to the definitive volumes of Strauss and Lehtinen (*Psychopathology and Education of the Brain Injured Child*, Volume I, Grune and Stratton, 1947) and Strauss and Kephart (*Psychopathology and Education of the Brain Injured Child*, Volume II, *Progress in Clinic and Theory*, Grune and Stratton, 1955). These pioneering authors stressed the need to recognize and appreciate *individual differences* in children (and therefore also adults) in the learning and behavioral disabilities. It follows, then, that there's a need for individualized instruction and management if we are to help these children academically and emotionally. This brings up a profound dilemma: on the one hand, careful diagnosis is required in order to institute appropriate remediation—educational, psychological, and medical; on the other hand, almost ever-present labeling attends and at times overwhelms the good intentions of diagnostic therapeutics.

Educational Handicap, Neurological Handicap, Learning Disability, Learning Lab, Pill to Increase His Attention Span—such terms are translated into Peerlanguia (language of buddies) and Environ-Gossipa (dialect of the neighborhood) as MR, stupid, retarded, nuts, bad, etc. and combinations thereof. The child and adult with minimal brain dysfunction who manifest learning problems in behavioral and/or cognitive areas need help. They stand out. As a matter of fact, the smarter they are the more they stand out and the more obvious their plight. And yet, even with the best intentions, they are not only evaluated and managed; they are also grouped and marked. It's turmoil if one doesn't get help; it's turmoil if one does. My only way out is a hedgy one: sensitive individualization of each youngster's difficulties is needed . . . taking into account all the organic and emotional subtleties . . . personal, familial, environmental. All the disciplines involved *should* be involved . . . but they shouldn't fight with one another. So that this youngster (and his family) in turmoil . . . has the best possible setting . . . educationally, psychologically, and medically . . . to help him cognitively and behaviorally . . . and yet maintain and even increase his self-concept and self-esteem. All this is nicely outlined but not so easy to do!

A last thought (for this chapter, of course): How much dysfunction does one have to have before we can call it damage? Even though they may coincide, I feel that the two are conceptually different and that five grams of the former will not really equal one gram of the latter. Historically, damage has had to be verified by pathological (anatomical) examination. In adults we can speak of damage because the clinical manifestations can be proved (at least from a correlative point of view) during surgery or at post mortem examinations. (Thank God we do not have to perform many autopsies on children.) This means that often the diagnosis of minimal brain dysfunction in children is inferred, presumptive, not proved, and also (depending on whom one is talking to) not there—a figment of the Learning Disabilitologist's imagination. Even though there is little anatomical evidence, from a practical point of view and with all of the historically corroborative data enumerated above, I feel fairly safe in indicating that the dyslexia and dysgraphia syndromes, the syndromes of motor-perceptual impairment, the hyperactivity-distractability and decreased attention span syndromes, and the language delays are based on dysfunction of the central nervous system. Later I will discuss some neurophysiological studies which tend to support this hypothesis. *Dysfunction* shows us what's happening in everyday life. Parents and children get very upset with the term *brain damage*. It has a connotative finality about it. I prefer and use the expression *dysfunction*. Sometimes I use the term *damage* when the symptoms and signs in an individual with minimal brain dysfunction clearly are intermingled with the symptoms and signs of the cerebral palsies, the epilepsies, the retardations, and/or blindness and deafness. But I use the term *damage* with great caution. Pragmatically as a practitioner I feel it is important to stress the *primary* organic, physical, neurological, physiological, biochemical, (at times even genetic) nature of the learning disabilities . . . and the *secondary* but important (sometimes *the* main problem, especially in older children) emotional and psychological sequelae—always remembering primary emotional problems which might arise from other sources . . . and always remembering the problems which might arise from social, economic, and cultural factors.

My organic bias is due in part to my fear that if a primary emotional and psychological cause is assigned to the learning disabilities, then tendencies in treatment might be started which in my judgment have been at times relatively ineffectual. And by delaying the "full" assessment . . . well? It isn't necessarily true that a little psychotherapy can't hurt anybody anyway. If the emotional environment is the cause of the child's learning problems . . . the emotional environment is almost always a euphemism for parents and that means *mother*, because she's around most of the time. And that means guilt, guilt, and more guilt. Not gilt, but guilt! The parents I know—especially parents of youngsters with learning problems—have plenty of guilt. They really don't need any more; actually the guilt kneads them. I spend a good bit of time, happily, in my office, trying to relieve guilt—most of it based on fantasy, very little of it based on actual performance. I could do a whole book just on the guilt feelings of mothers and fathers and patients too. And that is among the subjects of the next chapter.

Attention Deficit Disorder

Distractibility--- Hyperactivity---
Short Attention Span---
Limited Concentration Power---
Stimulus Bound---
The Kid with the Short Fuse...

Spiels I have sown, known, thrown, and at times (unfortunately) blown

Spiel I

I try to live the way I write; I like to kid around—even at serious moments. To me a good bit of life is tragi-comedy or comi-tragedy. It depends on when, what, who, how. I can open the morning paper and break up laughing. I can do a double-take and come back to the same headlines a few minutes later and burst into tears. Just with some stories, not with all of them.

When people laugh *with me*, I'm there. *At me*, that's another story. When one chooses to clown around, he takes that risk. In my daily interaction with people—home, office, market, tennis court, liquor store—if I can get them to smile, I win a little too. If the parent is clearly amused, often the child becomes more relaxed and we're all happier. The shtick backfires sometimes: Routine physical examination. A twelve-year-old. Some years ago. Mother in the examining room. I was in a good mood, a little slapsticky maybe. The youngster didn't break a smile. I used the best of my repertoire, in three languages yet. Intellectually, my patient was way up there . . . I could tell from our conversation and the reading material toted along. Losing, I said to both, "Some kids sure act grown-up." Mother replied, "And some grown-ups sure act like kids."

WHAP

Oh, well. So my first spiel is to try to get everyone in a good mood. But remember, in great part I'm doing it for me too. The origins of this approach stem from need—yea, almost adver-

73

sity: Many years ago. My first routine physical examination. I entered the room with appropriate flourish. I looked back to my nonexistent nurse . . . asking her to hold up all those imaginary calls. My cerebrum brimming with knowledge to impart, my soul aflame with compassion if required, I was ready to care for the physical, mental, and emotional needs of this 18-month-old infant . . . who, as I approached, began to . . . began to . . . cry? Yes! Cry! Cry! Cry! Also scream and fight! Ouch! Well, really now . . . was there a murmur? Forget it! Where was the heart? Was the spleen or liver enlarged? Who could feel the tummy within that twisting torso? How could I work in such a din? Poetry helps to cleanse the soul . . .

> And now I'm made to look the fool,
> They didn't teach *this* in medical school.

But good training pays off. I knew where to look it up! Thumbing excitedly through the indices of my *two* pediatric texts, I checked the "C's." But chagrin! Amazement! There was no heading "Crying—how to prevent" between "Cruveilhier-Baumgarten cirrhosis" and "Cryptococcosis." But then I smiled. How foolish of me. As with many important words in medicine, the German spelling probably persisted . . . so it would be listed under the "K's," no? . . . with "Kick—how to avoid baby's" . . . and "Kindergarten—how to fill out forms for." But alas! There was no "Krying" between "Kreb's Cycle" and "Kunkel's Syndrome."

It was then that I dedicated myself to that noble endeavor of attempting to prevent crying in the office (a primer is being written) and its logical corollary: to make people happy in the office.

Spiel II

Most children and adults come to me with varying degrees of concerns and anxieties, depending on: age of patient . . . how much the schools are worried . . . how much the parents are worried . . . how much the patient is worried . . . how much bugging has gone on . . . what Aunt Emma said on the phone from Roseville on St. Valentine's Day two years ago . . . about causes and management of it all, but especially about causes . . . "You know whose fault it really is, don't you?" sort of thing . . . what the patient has been told about learning problems . . . but especially what the patient has *not* been told about learning problems . . . because that allows, yea stimulates, all sorts of fantasies, usually *bad ones.* . . . (*Information-giving is a most important aspect in the management of learning disabilities.*)

After all, there's a very good chance that by the time a patient comes to our offices he or she has already been maligned with several epithets equivalent to hazy, crazy, and/or lazy. . . . The reactions of patients who come for the first time: "I don't know (he really doesn't) why I'm here today." . . . "I came for a physical examination even though I had one with Doctor Jones last month, didn't I?" . . . "I'm bad in school. You gonna fix it up?" . . . "I can't read. You gonna fix it up?" . . . "Doctor, may we speak to you privately, before you examine Johnny?" . . . And the one that even now tears me up a little bit every time I remember. He was about ten, curly brown hair, blue eyes, freckles. But he was so, so sad. . . . "I'm dumb," he said. . . . And the only time I was really afraid for my physical being in the office: . . . He was eighteen years old, big, strong, and angry! He had come with his father, by referral from a physician from a rural school district. But he was angry—very, *very* angry! He thought that the school thought that because he couldn't read, he was "nuts" and that I was the psychiatrist who was going to treat him. . . .

And so Spiel II usually goes like this: "Did you know this is the clinic for *smart* kids who still have a little trouble at school?" I repeat it . . . with enunciation and a little flair and a little smile. Then I ask the youngster to repeat it. They usually get it right, right away. If they're older I say, "You know, if you were younger, I'd say, 'Did you know this is the clinic for smart kids who still have a little trouble in school?' But since you're older, I don't say it. Get it?" They usually do.

There are many variations and ramifications of Spiel II, which I have to play by ear. I can't study this scenario; it's almost purely ad lib. Its main function is Not to Turn the Kid Off. He may well have been tested, retested, and supertested by several specialists. He may well have been counseled and recounseled and overcounseled by advisors etc., etc., etc. And he may well have *had* it! Enough of it! I would go on only if I felt that I could help, remembering one of my very few extant Latin phrases: *Primum non nocere*—"First don't hurt." It's bad enough that at times in the healing arts and sciences we can't help. But at least, "First don't hurt."

Then I go on, "I know you're smart, good, nice, and not lazy. Otherwise you couldn't have gotten into *this* clinic. There's another specialist down the hall who takes care of the dumb kids. But you couldn't get into that clinic. Dig?" They dig. "Now tell me what kind of trouble you're having in school and let's see what we can do to help, working together." During future visits, I ask our patients to repeat the words and nature of what I had hoped I emphasized. Usually, they do quite well.

Spiel III

This spiel has to do with the explanations I give for the discrepancies in performance . . . divergences in talent . . . dichotomies in potential and achievement . . . "disturbances" in behavior. . . .

I use my old buddy, *localization of function*. I ramble a bit: "Y'know, one of the troubles with the world today is the mistake many people make about the head, the brain. We used to think that the head was all good or all bad, all OK or all not OK, 100% smart or 0%—dumb. But . . . y'know . . . that's really not so. No, really. Research and science have proved it. The head has many parts and some can be working great (poor English, I know) and some ain't swinging so good." And then I put my palm on the youngster's head and move my fingers slowly about . . . decisively . . . to different skull areas. (Sort of like the hand of the physician is upon thee; a bit schmaltzy perhaps.) "This area is for seeing and this spot specializes in hearing, and this one is for music tones and there are two for reading. No kidding, two spots for reading . . . one on the left and the other on the right. There are at least two types of reading problems. Did you know that? You can be very smart and good and nice and not lazy and still have trouble in reading, because one of those two spots might be just a little weak, or might need some more time to develop and grow up. There's an area that controls spelling and one for writing and several spots for math and sports." Then, depending on the youngster's age and the emotional climate we have created, "This spot's for geometry, this one's for poetry appreciation, and this one's for understanding dirty jokes. It's hard for people to dig why, if you talk so nicely, you can't read well . . . or why, if you read so well, you can't sit still too long . . . or why, if you're such a whiz in art, you can't spell well . . . or why, if you're so good in sports, you have trouble with language."

Sometimes things work out well; at other times, my plans and hopes go awry. Usually, the patients who are easiest to work with are the adults who are interested in knowing why they have difficulties and then how they might overcome them or work around them. I have quite a few adult patients; each one could be the basis for a sensitive, instructive chapter. One man, dyslexic and dysgraphic in English and Spanish, came to our clinic because he was up for promotion in a local food store—from floor manager to office manager, with all the literate skills thereunto appertaining. One lady's greeting was, "I want you to help me to learn to read so that I can get a job and get off welfare." This lady not only came from a disadvantaged environment but in addition she had dyslexia and dysgraphia. She's so sharp that she memorized the Driver's Manual while a friend read it to her.

One of the most dramatic episodes began when I received a call from the medical ward for an *emergency* learning disability consultation. There was this patient with an acute bleeding ulcer. . . .

"Now wait a minute. This must be a mistake. I'm Dr. Rosenthal, the pediatrician and Learning Disabilitologist. Are you sure you want me?" "Yes, yes, specifically you!"

It turned out that this patient had been taunted in his early years because of reading, writing, and coordination problems . . . but was smart enough and sensitive enough to realize he was being taunted. He had to take a job which required no paper and pencil expertise . . . which he wasn't happy with. He had a very poor self-image. On the ward, he told his physicians how self-doubt and self-recrimination correlated with his abdominal pains (the emotional and stress factors in ulcer patients). Then came the bleeding episode and the hospitalization. . . .

My job was to explain what he didn't have . . . that he was not hazy, crazy, and/or lazy . . . then to explain what he did have . . . dyslexia, dysgraphia (at that time possibo-probably). . . . Later I was fairly sure. His general IQ was within normal limits. Then we started on remediation attempts. . . . One tip-off to the ward physicians is worth mentioning: *infrequently* do ulcers occur in non-high-powered types . . . this patient *seemed* by no means close to the "ulcer type" . . . but there was something else there. Luckily this patient had insight and spoke openly of his frustrations. . . .

The very young, up to ages seven, eight, nine, are still somewhat confused as to why such a fuss is made about school. They often come to our offices with mixed feelings of being perplexed and anxious (and thus afraid): "What are we here for?" "Another test!" "What do you mean, he knows about brains?" "But the teacher said I was doing better!" Etc., etc., etc.

Grades, class standing, achievement scores, and IQ tests generally have not dented their value systems yet, NOT ALWAYS

SO—I KNOW!! It depends in part on where you are. I know some first graders who can recite the class standing in reading and math day by day.

A very tough group are the youngsters from eight to fourteen. The need for peer group acceptance is great, and discrepancies in cognitive and/or behavioral function seem to stand out all the more. Many of these youngsters come to us with anxiety and hostility: "There's nothing wrong with me!" "I don't need another doctor. I already have one!" "You know I had an important basketball game this afternoon!" "I can read if I want to!" Etc., etc., etc.

Unfortunately, the tendency exists for derring-do behavior in this group as a compensation for accusations of cognitive and/ or behavioral incompetence. The defiance may be verbal, sign-like, or quite physical (one lad walked on the outside of a building on a dare).

Spiel IV

Spiel IV is to go into the life histories of those who made it big in spite of their school problems. A delightful source of information is the book by two English pediatricians Illingworth and Illingworth entitled *Lessons from Childhood* (Williams and Wilkins Co., 1966).

Alessandro Volta—pioneer of electricity—at first seemed dull-witted and was slow in learning to talk.

Albert Einstein was quite late in learning to talk. And when he was four, his parents were worried that he might be mentally backward—Einstein hated learning classical languages.

Henri Poincaré—the great mathematician—had trouble recognizing space and form. He was totally unable to make a draw- that represented anything recognizable in heaven or earth.

Napoleon had great difficulty with spelling and had terrible handwriting. In addition, he was quite awkward and clumsy as a boy. He couldn't throw, shoot, or ride well at all.

Beethoven—it was said that nothing fragile was safe in his clumsy hands.

Leonardo da Vinci wrote from right to left, reversing letters. (A friend of mine once said, "I should have such problems.")

Ben Franklin, Schubert, Emerson, Gogol, Wagner, Conan Doyle—all had marked troubles with math.

The Helen Keller-Anne Sullivan story, though perhaps not immediately relevant to learning disabilities, is a magnificent example of conquest over adversity through understanding and persistence.

Winston Churchill was always at the bottom of his class. Interestingly, his teachers saw him as backward and precocious *at the same time.* In our own experience, and perhaps related, is the fact that some children have qualified for the educationally handicapped program and the gifted program *at the same time!*

Edison was low man in his class, always. One day his teacher said that his mind was addled.

George Bernard Shaw always found spelling difficult and tried to spell in a phonetic manner.

Cézanne, Goethe, Rimski-Korsakov, Bismarck, Napoleon—all had unbridled tempers.

Hans Christian Andersen used to day-dream and paid little attention to his teachers. Macdonald Critchley, the English neurologist, feels that Andersen was a genuine example of a developmental dyslexic. Andersen clearly had no trouble with language expression (all those delightful fairy tales). But his written manuscripts in Danish in Copenhagen show the unmistakable errors of the dyslexic attempting to transform his thoughts into adequate graphic symbols (Macdonald Critchley in *Dyslexia*, edited by Keeney and Keeney, the C. V. Mosby Co., 1968). It would be interesting to know just how Andersen finally did get his thoughts published—I mean literally *how?* By a secretary taking dictation? Tape recorders didn't exist then.

An Unnamed Realtor I know, bright as can be, had mild reading and writing problems when in school. He married his reading tutor, got a dictaphone and several good secretaries, and it's been the road to success all the way.

Auguste Rodin is perhaps one of the outstanding embodiments of the well-endowed right-brained person—spatial, geometric, and relational. In his biography of Rodin, Bernard Champigneulle (Rodin, 1967, Harry N. Abrams, Inc.) emphasizes that as a student the great sculptor-to-be seemed retarded. Gross spelling errors pervaded his writing and he had great difficulty with Latin and mathematics. What a fortunate way out for a youngster with language weaknesses: to create masterpieces in a three-dimensional medium—sculpture!

The shikseh in *Portnoy's Complaint* (by Philip Roth, Random House, 1967) is another example.

CRITIC: "Oh . . . oh . . . Rosenthal's *really* flipped this time."

ROSENTHAL: "No . . . wait . . . gimme a chance."

CRITIC: "OK, just a few lines to explain before they come for you. Don't worry, we'll send you to a nice place to rest up. OK—write quickly now!"

Well, firstly, a shikseh is a non-Jewish girl (at least originally) who stands out as an objet de désir for certain Mediterraneanly descended boys. For those of us who read *Portnoy's Complaint* for reasons other than prurient, I believe a provocative diagnosis can be made in retrospect for the female protagonist—the Monkey. The author spends a great deal of time and employs a profusion of Anglo-Saxon monosyllabic expletives to delineate the young lady's physical charms. But all through the book she is portrayed as having perhaps less than an adequate IQ, mostly because of her reading and writing difficulties. And she pictures herself as being dumb with all the concomitant loss of self-esteem. On page 207 (my copy), the author describes how the Monkey must laboriously move her lips and mouth her words as she is scanning a page to help her read. On page 205 is a startling example of the Monkey's writing—a note to her cleaning lady which is about as phonetic a script as could be imagined. She seems to have little Gestalt or sight-see word concepts. Yet this girl is verbally bright, and the author leaves us with few doubts that her motor-coordinated efforts left little to be desired. At times in the book she is poignant in the expression of her self-doubts. *She knows she's dumb yet she's smart enough to realize it but not understand why.* Perhaps a diagnosis of dyslexia-dysgraphia? Perhaps indeed!

The trouble with many of the examples listed above like Alessandro Volta and Hans Christian Andersen is that they do not mean so much to a twelve-year-old as to us older folks. If there were a phenomenally successful rock music star or quarterback or movie heroine with a history of learning disabilities for our patients to emulate and identify with . . . that would help a great deal. Please step forward and volunteer.

Spiel V

This spiel has to do with successful adaptation, a subject I focus on in visits after the initial assessment.

Academically, I hope it goes this way: "What grade are you in now, John? Getting some special help in math, are you? I prefer our youngsters to be based in regular classes (to avoid labeling) and to be sent out for remedial help for some hours per week, if possible. Are you attending any special institutes or schools? How are the grades? Better? Good! Keep up the fine work. You're doing better, and you know that I know that you know it. Jumped six months in reading in three months? Great! 92% on the last math test? Terrific! Look at how that writing's improved! (The longing for a grade of A must be immense in these youngsters.) How's that sharp younger brother of yours doing? He'd *love* to catch up to you, but you'd rather keep the two-year-age-span between you clear, huh?"

But it doesn't always go this way.

Behaviorally, I hope it goes this way: "Jane, I think you're doing so well that we won't have to give you that medicine after all. Even if we do have to, it'll be like a crutch, and probably for a short while anyway. You really have a nice grip on yourself. And with those dancing classes after school, you're getting rid of that energy at the right times. You're certainly less distractible and you can concentrate much longer during class. Whether it's your age or maturation or social learning, I'm not sure. But you're getting there."

But it doesn't always go this way.

As for self-esteem, I hope it goes this way: "Do you like yourself more, Jimmie, now that you're doing better? Or are you doing better because you like yourself more? I mean in the sense of respect . . . you know, respect yourself more. Others certainly do. Look at the nice things the teachers are saying. I guess you have to respect and like yourself a little before you can feel that way about the world."

But it doesn't always go this way.

Socially, I hope it goes this way: "So you're in the Scouts now? Great. Lots of new friends, I bet. And you're getting along better with buddies now, huh? Trying to control that temper— win *or* lose, your way *or* their way. You know, what we used to call your "short-fuse." And David slept over last weekend and you're going to be his guest this weekend? Say, that's just great!

It's nice to have friends to share fun with . . . to know the pleasure of take *and* give."

But it doesn't always go this way.

As for nonacademic areas, I hope it goes this way: "So you exhibited your stamps at the last regional meeting, Bobbie? That's great! And you made up the designs and cut the matting yourself? And the printing—I heard about that printing! So many labels and titles! Terrific! And Julie's doing tap *and* ballet and is in the school show next Friday night? Wow! Can you really do a tap version of Swan Lake? That should be . . . novel. And George —first-string basketball and you read and memorized all those plays, even those with complicated sequences." (I have faith that nonacademic and academic successes will inter-generalize like Goodness Leadeth Unto Goodness.)

But it doesn't always go this way.

I Re-explain—I HOPE IT GOES THIS WAY:

I re-explain the natures and extents of the learning disabilities as per Spiels I, II, III, IV, and V. I play it by ear and stress what's needed in relation to the pressing issues at the time.

But it doesn't always go this way.

Spiel VI

In time, a part of my neurological examination has developed enough peripheral benefits to become a full-fledged spiel. I look at the retinæ of my patients' eyes at practically every visit, even visits that are essentially for counseling. By observing the optic nerves via this funduscopic examination I can at times evaluate possible increases in brain pressure and reassure myself that there is no objective evidence for such. Let me hasten to add that in all our some 1300 patients (oh, yes—between the early chapters and now, our number of patients has increased) I have never seen evidence of increasing intracranial pressure resulting, for example, from a mass like a tumor—which might have caused cognitive and/or behavioral changes. This is not to say that this is impossible; we are always on the alert for it. Also, because I feel that errors of omission are a somewhat greater sin than errors of commission, I have continued to look at the optic nerves. At any rate, the children used to ask me:

CHILD: "What are you looking at each time?"

ME: "Oh, just your optic nerves."

CHILD: "What's that?"

ME: "Well, it's like this . . . (five-minute explanation) . . . Do you understand?"

CHILD: "Not really."

Finally I got wise:

CHILD: "What are you looking at each time?"

ME: "Oh, that's part of your brain." (Since the optic nerve is a cranial nerve, it really is.)

CHILD: "Oh, how's my brain?"

ME: "Fine! Just fine!"

CHILD: "Oh, that's good. It's nice that you can see part of my brain and tell me that it's OK."

And that's how Spiel VI was born.

Spiel VII

This spiel has to do with getting on *Rosenthal's Therapeutic Triumph List*. No kidding! After awhile, when I sense that things are going well from the aspects of academics, behavior, self-esteem, social life, nonacademic pursuits, and understanding of self and problems (in short, when the parents and child seem to grasp that the troubles are due not to being hazy, crazy, and/or lazy but to subtle difficulties in cognition and/or behavior)—then I flamboyantly whip out several clipped sheets of paper. As excitement and speculation mount, I announce: "Since you're doing so well, you go on my list of *Therapeutic Triumphs!* That's for kids who are really making it." I did it, at first in a moment of slapsticky exuberance with two parents and a youngster who were delighting in their successful adaptation and substantial accomplishments. But then I realized that the *Therapeutic Triumph List* and the attaining of that distinction were therapy in themselves. I do feel that such a list has at least as much social significance as those that have to do with Best (or Worst) Fully Dressed . . . Best (or Worst) Scantily Dressed . . . Best (or Worst) Undressed. . . . Of course, through the years I have maintained a code of the strictest ethical aboveboardness. Never has the scandal of bribery to get on *Rosenthal's Therapeutic Triumph List* even been whispered.

Spiel VIII

This spiel has to do with the assiduous tracking down and stamping out of guilt—usually in parents, but also in patients and even in involved professionals. I refer here to feelings of guilt which are *unbased* and *undeserved* and which tend to *undo* and *unglue* parents so that they function much more *inefficiently* as they almost desperately attempt to help and console their children who are having problems at school and at home. I'm sure that through the years most parents must have made some errors and are entitled to a few feelings of self-doubt. But the guilt of which I speak is the feeling which wells up in people as a result of misunderstanding and misinformation—they tend to blame themselves. Others, at times, even help them along in those feelings. My purpose is not to whitewash humanity and absolve it from guilt and sin but rather to assess areas which are a bit vague.

I try to sense the guilt—both by type and by amount. At times, parents will quickly blurt it out. On other occasions they are tense and withholding. Guilt is generally of two types:

1. "What did we do wrong?"

2. "Did we do wrong when we did such and such a thing at such and such a time?"

I believe that a diagnosis of minimal brain dysfunction which is organically based with secondary emotional problems is easier for parents to take than a diagnosis of a primary emotional-psychogenic disturbance which causes learning and/or behavioral problems. A diagnosis like minimal brain dysfunction causes much less self-recrimination generally, because it tends to reduce the self-doubt inherent in guilt questions 1 and 2 above. The meaning I try to convey is that nothing or very little wrong was actually done to the child. Rather, the patient has these problems innately and neurophysiologically—essentially from birth. The formal activities of school usually, but not always, bring them out.

Guilt comes in other guises as well: When I was in practice but a few years a mother came to my office with a little boy who had a respiratory illness. . . . "Is it asthma? Or bronchitis?" she asked. Her voice trembled. . . . I knew that one was *really* bad and the *wrong* answer. . . . *But which one?* A 50/50 chance. . . . Somebody had probably told her that one of these diagnoses was destined to cause great and chronic disability . . . and that it probably came from *her side* of the family. . . . I had *a 50/50 chance.* . . . My voice trembled, "Asthma?". . . . "Oh, my God," she despaired. . . . "Oh, my God," I despaired. . . . Then I said, "How about bronchitis?". . . . She said, "No! No! You're just trying to make me feel better.". . . Then I said, "How about asthmatic bronchitis?" (Which it really was.) To no avail. I couldn't expiate her guilt. I had failed.

But on another occasion, I sailed. During a learning disability assessment . . . I take a full history:

ME: "How was the prenatal course?"

MOTHER: "Fine, Doctor. No trouble at all."

ME: "And the delivery? Full-term and all OK?"

MOTHER: "Oh, yes, quite easy and Jerry weighed seven and a half pounds."

ME: "And now, how about . . . "

MOTHER: "Of course, I know I shouldn't have taken that long a bus trip when I was only three months pregnant."

ME (having to shift cognitive gears back to the prenatal course): "What do you mean?"

MOTHER: "Well, *I know* Jerry's reading problems and hyperactivity are due to that long bus ride I took to Pennsylvania at that time—six thousand miles back and forth. But I couldn't help it. My father was very sick and I just had to go. We didn't have enough money for me to fly, so I had to go by bus. And then I read in that magazine about long car trips when you're pregnant and school troubles with the children later on. But what could I do?"

ME: "Did you hemorrhage or have a threatened miscarriage or . . . ?"

MOTHER: "Oh, no . . . just that long ride."

(Not often does the opportunity for instant deification occur so fortuitously, but one must rise to the occasion and accept that distinction with the utmost of grace and humility. I did!)

ME: "My dear lady . . . there is absolutely no relationship that I know of between 'just long bus rides' when you're pregnant and trouble at school for the children later on."

MOTHER (she smiled and *was* relieved): "I *always* worried about that. I'm glad to know it wasn't my fault."

I was still playing that role when I got home that evening:

ME: "Honey it's *me. Zeus* is home. Mogen David on the rocks and my brown suede clogs please. Hup, two, three, four!"

SHE: "Zeus is it now?"

She hadn't had such a good day—OI VEY—and for me the fall from Olympus was quick and sure.

As a Parthian shot against the somberness of the guilt shtick, permit me to relate a strategem wherein we turn a guilt ruse to good use. We all have to—want to—lose weight because . . . well . . . it's fashion. With the best of intentions we starve at breakfast, deny ourselves at lunch. But it's the dinner and the subsequent nibbling that usually does us in. Just before I go home, I engorge about 100 calories worth of gooey-gushey chocolate! I've done well in losing weight and the reasons are probably twofold:

1. I'm riddled with premeditated self-created guilt and that really curbs my evening appetite.

2. Also, with chocolate on an empty stomach I'm a little nauseated.

RIPP—

a stunning new acronym on scholarship's horizon:

Reassuring
Informative
Pre
Psychotherapy

BY APPROPRIATE AND TIMELY INFORMATION-GIVING –
TO *PREVENT* PSYCHOPATHOLOGY

The information-giving aspect of our learning disability evaluation is at times the most important service we can offer. It can:

> discourage doubts . . .
>
> dispel disquietude . . .
>
> disavow demons of despair.

Again we play it ad lib. Informative prepsychotherapy is offered to patients individually, to parents, to patients and parents, and to groups. The first I try to play down; the last two are the most fun and probably the most productive. I attempt to have the patient and both parents together for several reasons:

- We're not dealing with hush-hush sins . . .

  Parents do get involved and are interested in their chil-
- dren. During regular examinations I prefer a parent to be present as part of the assessment and advice patterns. No child or adolescent should really be an island unto himself, I think . . .

- And, so that the information doesn't get churned, chopped, and changed into something that it wasn't originally.

Examples

ME: "There might be a physical basis to Johnny's hyper-active behavior."

(Two hours and three interpretations later)

SOMEBODY: "The doctor said it was brain damage!"

ME: "Dyslexia is probably a built-in problem with the de-coding of graphic or written symbols."

(Two hours and three interpretations later)

SOMEBODY: "The doctor said it was a type of retardation."

ME: "Auditory sequencing problems can occur even after passing a standard hearing test."

(Two hours and three interpretations later)

SOMEBODY: "The doctor says that Billy's putting us on. He can hear if he wants to."

I try to keep the family together as a unit—also from the information-giving aspect. Siblings, when of appropriate ages, should know of learning disabilities so that they can understand and show compassion for their troubled brothers and sisters. This is not always easy. Siblings tend to complain about the "special considerations" the troubled youngsters are getting. Siblings tend to see more guile and less cerebral dysfunction in the difficulties our patients have. (I'll get into this a little later when we discuss the "Can't-Won't" dilemma.) If all involved can hear the same story at the same time, it should cut down on misinterpretation and misunderstanding. If the dialogue is open and open-ended.

We often invite the parents and teachers of our patients as well as other professionals in small groups of ten to twenty to cozy, informative discussions. We have a comfortable meeting room at our Health Center and, as coffee is being served, I start off with some earthy humor (the vasectomy clinic is meeting in the next room). I stopped my dance routines for several reasons. Using slides, we present the concept of the Continuum of Psycho-biological Development, the definition of the Minimal Brain Dys-functions, and examples of dyslexic-dysgraphic writing, to mention only a few topics. I stress that the information we give is also supposed to stimulate conversation and controversy—and indeed it does. Our meetings are usually divided into two two-hour sessions a week apart. Many participants have asked to come back again. We also have an audio-visual program entitled Learning Disabilities Parts I and II. Each of the two tapes takes one hour and can be seen-heard by appointment at our Health Center. Participants are often relieved to know that others with the same problems exist:

"If there are so many of us, we can't be that different or abnormal."

"If there are so many of us, we have group strength."

Indeed, a great deal of mutual support evolves from these get-togethers, often with tangible extra goodies. These have to do with the ever-present question of how to deal with this problem *now*—at the time the problem comes up. Often the problems are behavioral and at home. "I don't want philosophy, Doc. I need immediate practical solutions of a mechanical-technical nature . . . now. In short, Doc, I want to survive." In part, I think of myself as a collator of information and a scribe. Sometimes I have specific advice; sometimes I'm forced reluctantly to fall back on clichés. And when that happens, we all know it. But when we throw the *specific* problems open to the group, marvelously *specific* solutions are sometimes forthcoming because the parents and teachers have been there and have lived it and by bruise-and-bear survival methods have come up with some winners.

Just an example a mother related to me once: It was a cold, depressing Saturday afternoon . . . Mother felt down in the dumps. Enter the fifteen-year-old daughter. . . . Daughter bursts through the door. . . . Daughter down in the dumps . . . it had been a bad week at school . . . reading was down . . . attention span short. . . . Mother and daughter glower at each other . . . a crucial, delicate moment. It can go either way. . . . Mother recollects her cool and says: "Shall we dance?" . . . They both break up uproariously laughing . . . the afternoon and probably the weekend are spared, even saved. . . .

Humor, that great therapist, Lord, does it help! It's the only thing we've got left sometimes.

Then we continue in our approach to the minimal cerebral dysfunctions by discussing some of the more frequent symptoms and signs:

- Hyperactivity-distractability (decreased attention span)
- Perceptual-motor impairments: small-muscle dysfunctions and large-muscle dysfunctions (general coordination deficits.
- Dysfunctions of cognition and memory: auditory and visual sequencing problems
- Emotional lability and impulsivity
- Special learning disabilities: reading (dyslexia), arithmetic (dyscalculia), writing (dysgraphia, distinguished from poor small-muscle coordination), spelling
- Soft neurological findings: crossed dominance (small-muscle incoordinations, hopping difficulties, associated movements
- Disorders of language, speech, and hearing

Unfortunately, these symptoms and signs are not mutually exclusive. Any one or combination of them can exist. Maturational principles, as indicated before, should be kept in mind. Yet it is difficult to delineate when maturation sort of stops and a learning disability based on minimal cerebral dysfunctioning persists. Diagnosis and labeling always seem to be at odds with one another. We need good functional descriptions of the problems so that interprofessionally we can begin to understand one another—and so that we can understand the patients and their parents. Our ever-present attempts to discover a cause in order to explain to our patients the reasons why—as well as for scientific advancement—also engender the need for diagnosis. Yet diagnosis leads to labeling with all the evils thereunto appertaining. I know that such terms as Educationally Handicapped, Neurologically Handicapped, Learning Disabled, and Minimal Brain Dysfunction are often translated as stupid, MR, retarded, lazy, nuts, etc. But I don't really know what to do about it. Except to explain these terms adequately, honestly, and correctly to the world, the community, the peers, the friends, the family, the siblings, the parents, and the patient. So let's try the best we can.

Take, for example, the syndrome of hyperactivity-distractability (decreased attention span). I will first (cleverly) not try to define it, but describe it:

"Johnny is motion itself."

"He won't sit still or is it that he can't?"

"Even at night he's not quiet. You should see the blankets in the morning."

"He always gets into fights on the playground."

"She day-dreams . . . yes . . . but still is very distractible."

"When we're together . . . with no distractions . . . Sally follows my directions quite well. But in a class of thirty—oh my!"

"He's always falling out of his seat." (Coordination problems may contribute to this.)

"If a car goes past the window, Jimmy's eyes go past his book."

"He twists in his seat so much, I'm afraid he'll go through its back like a whirlpool some day."

"He gets frustrated so easily."

"She's up and down—always!"

"He's in and out—always!"

"Does he wander about the room!"

"She's here and there always!"

"Attention span doesn't exist."

"Concentration power? Like two minutes!"

"She constantly bothers the other children."

"He makes so much noise in his seat that I had to place a rug under it to cut down the vibrations on the wooden floor."

"His unpredictability is almost predictable."

"Academic improvement followed the placing of one empty seat all around Mike."

"I am *not* distractable! . . . I'm *distracted*!"

"He makes guttural sounds for no reason."

"Always tapping his fingers and feet."

"She giggles and wiggles."

"He jiggles and wriggles."

"Does *he* have a short fuse!"

"Changes in routine upset him."

"He seems to be distracted by the flow of his own thoughts."

"Yes, Billy bounces about a good deal in school . . . but we also have problems on holidays at home with so much family around. And lunch rooms and restaurants are tough . . . he just doesn't seem to be able to handle all those stimuli. So we usually try to get him to eat lunch at home and we push to have as many picnics as possible."

The conceptual bias (not prejudice) I would like to present is that hyperactivity-distractability are indeed behavioral problems based on minimal cerebral dysfunctioning but that there are also environmental factors which play decisive roles in eliciting such behavior. In addition, the concept of the continuum comes to the fore—that is, how much hyperactivity-distractability does one have to have, not so much to acquire the diagnosis as to be in need of help because of unacceptable conduct?

If we note a youngster who can't seem to sit still, who is always on the move, who talks out of turn, who is distractable and distracting, who has a short attention span, who has excessive ups and downs, who has frequent tantrums, who has a short fuse, who has short concentration, who. . . . Wait! Wait a minute! Relative to what? By what criteria do we say *such* things about *some* youngsters? Well, it seems that from a practical point of view, if one has hyperactivity-distractability, it relates to what most of the other youngsters in the class are like (or rather are *not* like). Sure there are activity meters that measure motoric output and I'm certain we could build a distractometer. But usually statements are based on subjective and relative measures. Still, youngsters with hyperactivity-distractability have trouble making it in their environments. Several years ago, most of the problems had to do with these youngsters making unacceptable waves. These problems still exist. But we are now also getting referrals like: "If he could just sit still long enough. . . . If she could just tune out the irrelevant then he and she could read better, etc., and jump their grades." That is, we are now getting as many referrals for *intrakid* as for *interkid* problems. But there are many variables and determinants:

age

enough rest?

time of day

day to day

maturational factors

motivational factors

1 to 1 as opposed to 30 to 1 situations

how many similar kids are around?

incipient illness

before or after a meal

his best friend left for Los Angeles

her best girlfriend started dating her best boyfriend

fear of getting punished

heavy allergy history?

But also: What "type" (to be explained) of teacher is involved? . . . Often heard in different ways: "How come the first grade teacher didn't find him hyperactive and the second grade teacher does?"

In the point-counterpoint of life, the teacher with her or his neurophysiological and psychological makeup must blend with the neurophysiological and psychological makeups of twenty, thirty, or forty students. When anecdotal, but frequent, evidence comes to us that some teachers can take one or even two or three hyperactive-distractable children in a class (unless the class itself is upset) while other teachers "can't," then the latter are accused of being "old-fuss and fashioned," "psychologically rigid," and even "undemocratic" while the former are "modern-loose," "permissive," and even "a little too liberal." My hypothesis is that the determinants are less psychological and political than physiological. Teachers, like physicians, like pro ballplayers, like milkmen, like masseuses, like delicatessen owners, are all part of that homo sapiens bunch and have neurophysiological makeups as well as psychological ones. Of course, I suspect that certain "personality types" (neurophysiologically based?) tend to drift to certain workstyles. A mother once earnestly asked for help because, although she understood that her youngster was organically overactive and although she was quite motivated and desirous of helping him, she just couldn't cope with him. That youngster started walking at ten months of age. And his mother's been running ever since. She wants to cope. But she *can't* (I believe *neurophysiologically* so). I don't think she needs psychotherapy. I do think she can use a rest, help in the house, and a candlelight dinner for two at Pierre's—not infrequently. (Permit me, Madame, Monsieur, to recommend the spécialité de la maison—Pierre's own gefilte fish.)

I do believe and suggest that it is the *initial* neurophysiological state which permits or does not permit a person—child or
adult—to collect, connect, corral, collate, and coordinate . . .
coolly (successfully) . . . all the stimuli . . . visual, auditory, tac-
tile, and even kinesthetic . . . which can be thrown at a body and
mind . . . with thirty children and one teacher in a room. . . .
sure, there are secondary emotional problems!

It's almost as though the hyperactivity were really a reaction of the body (like fever)—a desperate attempt to pull together
all the sights, sounds, touches (others' and one's own) to make
some sense of it all, to make it livable-with.

That's why—probably—we don't see hyperactivity-
distractability in the physician's office too frequently. For two
reasons:

1.   The youngster is anxious, even scared, and I hear him
      think: "Just twenty more minutes to go. Just till the
      appointment's over with. Then I can move around a
      little . . . but only then. I'll just keep this grip on my-
      self a little longer."

2.   The physician's office presents close to a 1 to 1 rela-
      tionship. There are usually not many distracting per-
      ipheral stimuli floating around.

Yet some youngsters will at times even show hyperactivity in
what is perhaps one of the warmest, closest, most personal, 1 to 1
relationships of modern times—between man and his TV set.

Distractability is more of an intrakid problem.

Hyperactivity is more of an interkid problem.

Generally, the criterion seems to be that there is enough
quantitative difference between these children and the rest of us
to make them, from a practical point of view, *"outstanding"* and
in trouble with their peers and themselves. Most teachers I know
try heroically not to label these youngsters. But there seems to
be a need to abbreviate long, functional descriptions into diagnostic categories. If only the world understood the limitations
of the labeling and realized that wonderful things can happen
with time, development, teaching, understanding, love—and not
hurling accusations of hazy, crazy, and/or lazy. And wouldn't it
be great if we all meant the same thing when we used the same
term—and we all used the same term when we meant the same
thing?

In order to teach successfully, some structure in the class is necessary. But I know we could discuss for days the meaning of "teaching," "teachable," "structure," "order," "disorder," and so forth. These youngsters with hyperactivity and distractability tend to disturb this structure and themselves. It "seems" (I'll explain later) that they start the day, let us say, with 100 ergs of energy. They've got to get rid of it. When they're older they sense (either through maturation or social learning or both) where, when, and how they can successfully and socially-acceptably blow the steam:

Johnny: Monday Plan

Ride bike to school—hard!	10 ergs
English—cool it—"strict teacher"	5 ergs
Math—a little looser	7 ergs
Gym—let 'er rip!	20 ergs
Lunch—eat, but move around	10 ergs
Science—lots of lab, volunteer a lot	10 ergs
History—late in the day, hold the squirms	5 ergs
After school basketball!	20 ergs
Bike home—hard!	10 ergs

3 ergs left—poor Mom! And Dad, and sibs, and Johnny. . . .

But first let's go back a bit. There are many causes of restlessness in the classroom which have to be considered in differential diagnosis:

anxiety for primary emotional reasons

fear, humiliation, worry, pain

"over-permissive upbringing"—"poor discipline"

early stages of illness

hunger (missed breakfast)

pin worms (causing anal itching)

hyperactivity-distractability based on minimal cerebral dysfunctioning (organic steam)

And so forth. Moreover, combinations of these causes are possible.

Generally, if a youngster has the outstanding behavioral symptoms and signs of hyperactivity-distractability to the point where he's making such waves that he's upsetting the class or where, by producing too many stimuli, the class is upsetting him, something should be done for all concerned. Two approaches have been used:

1.   Change the environment to decrease the stimuli

2.   Help the child to be less responsive to irrelevant stimuli, so that he can attend to the task at hand

The first approach, changing the environment, includes the following measures (not all of them are always possible):

Smaller classes

More teachers

Individualized instruction

Frequent breaks to blow steam

Allow the child to go home for lunch (although this maneuver labels him)

Cut down on visual and auditory distractions in the classroom: fewer windows, fewer wall displays, soundproofing

Structure the classroom. There *is* a difference between structure and repression

I'm consistently amazed by the amount of visual material presented on the walls of our classrooms—collages at times of awe-producing proportions. I think it might be difficult for many children to concentrate with all those multicolored eye-catching interests tempting them: life-size singing alphabets; the workings of the steam engine, part by part; the San Andreas Fault; the mating habits of boa constrictors. . . . When the heat is on at our home and our three boys just can't make it in peace and harmony, we banish them to the ends of the house. It's not a big house, but it's sort of a five-pointed star shape—exile points, in a manner of speaking. After some time without stimulation, they're begging to be good if they can just see other folks again, even their brothers and parents.

To be sure there's need for social contact—

But with flailing elbows

We also need a social contract.

Other good physical outlets which might also be used for building self-esteem include all sorts of sports—swimming, track, and so on. I like punching the bag. This really allows one to get rid of it, especially if one imagines appropriate faces on the bag. And drumming. It's really quite intriguing how many of our bouncy youngsters take to the drums. When one is stuck in the subway or during long examinations, I suggest isometric exercises. But be ready to explain your grimacing to a perhaps uninformed public.

And now we come to the second approach: helping the child to attend to relevant stimuli if maturation and environmental controls do not work. Unfortunately, there are pressing time factors. The child's unacceptable behavior may force the school to shorten his day, to allow attendance for only a half-day, or, finally, to have him taught at home. There *is* an emergency when parents are told at 2:00 PM that Johnny cannot come back to school unless something is done by tomorrow.

I don't know much about behavior modification techniques, except that some professionals have told me that sometimes they work.

Many different medicines have been tried. For some years now, central nervous system (CNS) stimulants have been effective as therapy in *some* children. *This has been a very hot issue.* In all fairness a headline that states "DRUGS USED TO DULL SCHOOL CHILDREN; DAMPEN CREATIVITY" could also read "CNS STIMULANTS FOUND IN SOME CHILDREN TO INCREASE ATTENTION SPAN; ENHANCE CREATIVITY."

Allow me quickly to mention some statistics. Of the 1300 patients in our learning disabilities clinic (let's say 1000, shall we? It's easier for me to work with mathematically) about 50% (or 500) have behavioral problems as part of the school trouble. About 50% of those (or 250) ever come to therapy by CNS stimulants. But in only about 50% of those cases (or 125) is the medical therapy considered successful. And it is used for limited periods. That's 125 of 1000 patients (or 12½%) for specific, limited amounts of time. In order for me to write a prescription for a CNS stimulant, at least five people have to agree that its possible advantages might outweigh its possible disadvantages: teacher(s), both parents, patient, and me.

This is still a very hot issue. For those of us who believe that minimal cerebral dysfunctioning can cause the behavioral difficulties associated with the hyperactivity-distractability syndromes, the fact that a CNS stimulant has been effective in some patients and not in others—why, indeed, it may even excite some —has been an enigma. CNS stimulants given to "normal" patients for other therapeutic reasons tend to excite them. Yet such stimulants tend to "calm," "relax," or "quiet down" some hyperactive and distractable patients. A paradox.

The clinical criteria for the selection of children who might benefit from CNS stimulants are not entirely satisfactory. Patients may be sluggish, yet distractable. The mode of action of the drugs is not clear. J. H. Satterfield and M. E. Dawson (1971) have found that in general the children who respond favorably to CNS stimulants tend to have high skin resistance and high EEG power in the 0-to-8-Hz frequency band.* Interestingly, this suggests a syndrome of *underarousal*. One possibility might be that the CNS stimulant-responsive child is *underaroused* neurophysiologically in much the same way as a fatigued, sleep-deprived person. His attention is therefore diffuse and unfocused, and his ability to cope with stress is impaired. Like the overtired, sleep-deprived two-year-old who has been kept awake a couple of hours past bedtime, he is often clinically hyperactive, yet neurophysiologically fatigued. CNS stimulants could help by increasing arousal or attention, thereby aiding the patient to attend to relevant stimuli while being able to tune out those that are irrelevant. Thus, the "paradoxical" effect of CNS stimulants in some hyperactive-distractable patients may be 'explained by an error of hypothesis: the observer has placed the patient incorrectly on an "arousal scale."

It is probably true that, clinically and functionally, most hyperactive-distractable patients are far to the right on an activity scale:

Activity Scale (Clinical-Functional)

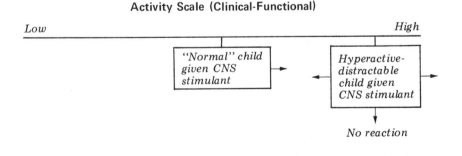

*J. H. Satterfield and M. E. Dawson, *"Electrodermal Correlates of Hyperactivity in Children,"* Psychophysiology 8 (March 1971), 191-197.

When a CNS stimulant is successful in the treatment of the hyper-active-distractable patient, it causes a shift to the left along the activity scale. When it fails therapeutically it causes no shift or a shift still further to the right. A shift to the right often results when a CNS stimulant is given to the "normal" child for other therapeutic reasons. However, on an arousal scale based on neuro-physiological measures, the picture may be surprisingly different:

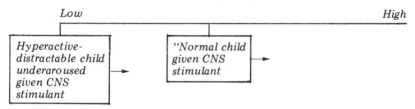

Arousal Scale (Neurophysiologically Based)

Low   *High*

Hyperactive-distractable child underaroused given CNS stimulant

"Normal child given CNS stimulant

The hyperactive-distractable patient may actually be under-aroused. Such a patient is far to the left on the arousal scale. When successful, therapy with a CNS stimulant causes a shift to the right in this patient, just as a stimulant often does in the normal child when given for other therapeutic reasons.

Under the direction of Professor Enoch Callaway, Chief of Research at the Langley Porter Neuropsychiatric Institute, University of California Medical Center, San Francisco, the responses of hyperactive-distractable children to CNS stimulants and place-bos are being studied by means of electroencephalographic aver-aged evoked cortical potentials. I hope that these physiological studies will yield a more rational basis for understanding these behavioral syndromes, and perhaps will enable us to predict which children in need might respond to which medicines and perhaps even in what doses.

Let's jump down the list a bit to Emotional Lability and Impulsivity. It is difficult—very difficult—when we are dealing with these "personality" variables to distinguish organicity from psychogenicity. Yet the distinction is important because different causes demand different treatments. But one thing is pretty ob-vious: that a hyperactive, distractable, emotionally labile, im-pulse-ridden child will shake up, irritate, and cause reactive hos-tility in those around him who don't understand (or are not willing to believe) that, at least originally, the child couldn't help it. Everybody around him accuses, needles, slings epithets at, and gives it but good to this troubled youngster. The environment might even destroy this child by setting standards of behavior he or she *can't* adhere to. But it's not the environment's "fault" either. Because there's limited room for "flailing elbows," especially in high-density areas like schools. The social contract, which the hyperactive-distractable youngster didn't really sign himself but which he is bound to live by, is being rattled. This child, realizing he is in the midst of a hostile milieu, is bright enough to "give it back." And after a while, it's very difficult to distinguish what were originally purposeless, uncontrollable random movements from what later became quite purposeful and provocative maneuvers intended to unnerve those occupying his life space. Antisocial and openly aggressive actions are, unfortunately, all too common in these children later on, especially in those who are hyperactive-distractable and dyslexic. I find, sadly, that I am writing a great many letters of evaluation and explanation to social and correctional agencies as well as to schools—for youngsters who have reached their teens.

There comes a time for the presentation of the Can't-Won't philosophy—not a spiel, really, because the light-heartedness is somewhat limited. Our patients, especially when they are older, create wide differences of opinion in surrounding adults. About one youngster a mother said: "I wish the teacher would stop bugging him! He has dyslexia and *can't* read any better. He's trying as hard as he can." About the same youngster, his teacher said: "I know he has dyslexia, but I feel he's leaning on it! I think it's mostly lack of motivation and that he *won't* try harder." Or a teacher will puzzle about another youngster: "I'm not sure if she *can't* or *won't* pay attention." Which is it? Or is it perhaps a combination of both? And if it is a combination—how much of each?

I usually ask the parents to be present: so that we can all communicate at the same time . . . so that they can reinforce what was said at a later time. ME (to the patient): "There's only one person who really knows the difference between the Can't and the Won't in himself. What's that? That's right: you. And let me tell you something else. Even *you* yourself don't know all the time. I sometimes talk to myself in the mirror. That's the Me-Me talking to the Mirror-Me and I say to myself: 'I really gave it all I had (whatever it was I was doing). I really did. I tried as hard as I could. No kidding . . . really.' But then I sometimes see the Mirror-Me give me a little look and then a smile—not sneakily, but quizzically. I'm not even sure about myself all the time, I guess. Johnny, you do the best you can. That's a full-time honorable job."

Perceptual-motor impairments have to do with a not-too-well-defined group of disabilities:

which are also on a continuum from better to worse . . .

which have maturational components . . .

which are essentially problems of integrating movements of different body parts . . .

and which have to do with troubles in being able to put it all together.

For me, the tennis serve is the undisputed zenith of all body parts efficiently working together—either to smash or curve the opponent to defeat. Also, it's the first series of motions (except for warmup) that the "watchers" (lots of girls, too) see you carry out. *It has to be good.* But even more—it has to *look good*! Form, form, form—from my old days on the basketball courts—that's what counts. Effectiveness, one can worry about after this other reputation is established. But so many things can go wrong with the serve because of the absolute need for smooth integration of so many body parts—237 at least! Permit me to mention some from head to toe:

Body Part	Function	Dysfunction
Brain: Frontal Lobe (Thinking Area)	To remember all the pro said	Poor night's sleep, worrying about next day's match
Brain: Motor Area	To serve to weak backhand	Inebriation
Eyes	To guide the racquet	Side-glancing at that gorgeous chick's half-volley in the next court
Hands	To grip the racquet	Chapped from doing the dishes
Lips	To smile the the psyching smile of imminent defeat for your opponent.	Cold sores

Body Part	Function	Dysfunction
Torso	To lean over the ball so the weight of your body is behind it	Overabundant periumbilical adipose tissue (big belly)
Large Toe	To inch up on, for height and trajectory	Gout

Some youngsters and adults have difficulties in subtle areas like right and left (laterality problems can be seen on the football field: one patient had trouble remembering which end the ground attack was to roll over), and difficulties in up-and-down, part-whole, and figure-ground discrimination. Their eye-hand coordination or visual-motor integration or motor-perceptual functioning is troubled. They have poor size, touch, space, distance, and even time discrimination and orientation. They have trouble knowing where their bodies are in space. They're not sure where they end and objects in space begin. It's not vision; they pass their eye examinations. It's perception: the brain's interpretation of what the eyes see. In order to get around tables and chairs they often have to touch them to be sure that they clear them adequately. With such inanimate objects there are upsets enough. But imagine a lunch line with Joey, Georgie, Mary, and Susie holding trays and Johnny has to get around that line by touching, almost bumping into *very animate* and subsequently quite *animated* beings—who don't really understand why Johnny is the way he is. Johnny gets labeled a "toucher"; "he always pushes"; "he leans on you." These youngsters also have trouble knowing where their body parts are in relation to themselves. That's when the milk and graham crackers end up by the right ear rather than in the mouth. Before age five, within the family framework, compensations can be made. But at school, even with understanding, there's a good bit of cleaning up to do and reactive unfriendliness from the environment. They have trouble translating data from the world into meaningful solidities they can lean on.

Small-muscle problems are seen in pasting, cutting, scissoring, shoelace tying, banana peeling, buttoning, tangerine dismantling, and writing. But there is a difference between small-muscle troubles in writing and dysgraphia, which has to do with problems in putting one's clear thoughts into appropriate graphic equivalents. Unfortunately, some youngsters have both. At times, mild uncontrolled motor movements of an athetoid or choreiform pattern might be noted.

Large-muscle dysfunctions (general coordination deficits) are present in youngsters who, through the years, have been thought of as awkward or clumsy. Many more insulting epithets have been their burden as well. These youngsters and adults tend to display rigid movement patterns—almost as though they have learned to work around a motoric sequence which has been difficult for them. Patterned movements can be seen in swimming, diving, running, playing baseball, and other activities. In time, things get better or less obvious or both. I'm not sure if it's mostly maturation of (working through) or successful compensation for (working around) the motoric confusion. I do feel that a great deal of help is given these youngsters by occupational therapists, who do refined diagnosing and prescribe specific motor exercises for specific motor dysfunctions. In taking a past history, delayed motoric development is sometimes noted.

As for soft neurological findings, some years ago the word *soft* was written as "soft," implying that the concept of soft neurological findings was soft indeed and even soggy. Well, with bravado, brazenness, and perhaps a little braggadocio, I have swept away the ignominious quotation marks. I submit that soft stands as hard data. These children are not blind, deaf, retarded, epileptic, or cerebral-palsied. But on careful and expanded neurological examination, positive findings, albeit soft, can be found:

slight differences in motor power on one side

trouble using a pencil

trouble copying designs

poor hand grip, one side or both

slight differences in reflexes on one side

not knowing one's own right and left

not knowing the examiner's right and left

troubles with finger to thumb apposition

difficulties with rapid alternating hand movements (adiadokokinesis)

hopping difficulties, one side or both

difficulties in crossing the midline with chalk on a blackboard

troubles in tandem walking

past-pointing, own finger to own nose or own finger to moving object subtle torso dysequilibriums

associated movements (trouble in getting the left hand to cool it while the right hand is doing a brain-ordered job)

mixed dominance: left-handed and left-footed but right-eyed; right-handed but left-footed and left-eyed

This last "finding" is sort of based on the notion that cerebral maturity and lateral dominance, especially to the right, correlate. I do know that there is a higher incidence of mixed dominance in youngsters with learning problems. What the significance is, I'm not sure. I do remember, however, when I was a young lad, that to be able to "hook shot" in basketball *with either hand* was probably the *greatest* athletic and therefore also social accomplishment—at any rate in my gang in Hester Street Park. Contrast this joy to the woe that left-handers face when they learn that the words "left" and "sinister" originally had the same meaning. Perhaps as an extension of the above-mentioned neurological examination, there should be an addendum—either by the examiner or by another competent observer. This special view assesses how Johnny is functioning in his daily life style:

in a class with thirty others . . .

listening to the teacher give dictation . . .

dodging paperclips from Jimmy's trusty rubber band . . .

writing down the spelling words . . .

sticking his tongue out at Mary . . .

trying to trip Sam as he walks by . . .

scraping the gum off his other shoe . . .

and remembering what his mother said about being good.

That is, the total brain-body-environment interaction.

As for electroencephalographic findings, these represent recordings of electrical activity from different parts of the brain. There is a good deal of argument inter- and intra-professionally about their value in the diagnosis and treatment of the minimal brain dysfunctions. The incidence of electroencephalograms (EEGs) which are not within normal limits is probably greater among children with school problems than among "normal" children. However, no correlations have yet been shown between certain types of EEGs and specific subdiagnoses of children with learning disabilities. At times, certain EEG findings indicate a drug of choice if behavioral problems are of such a nature that medication is being considered. Sophisticated, computerized EEG studies are now underway in several research institutions, especially with hyperactive and dyslexic youngsters, in an effort to define the underlying neurophysiology.

As for dysfunctions of cognition and memory, the common denominator of this group has to do with discrepancies and divergences in thinking. There are many types of cognitive talent—some can be great while others can be peculiarly inefficient. But with the understanding of and the belief in *localization of function*, the "why" can be explained. Some patients are delightfully bright, yet can't process auditory data into a meaningful sequence. For example, if three or four verbal requests are made in order, such a person can manage to remember in sequence only one or two. These youngsters and adults are not deaf or stupid or uncooperative: they have problems with auditory sequencing.

Visual sequencing abilities are quite basic to successful reading comprehension. I have been told by some patients that as they read past the first eight or nine words in a sentence, they must go back to the beginning again because they've lost the sequential meaning of the words. There are differences in short-term and long-term memory, and probably also in first- and second-language learning. Abstract and concrete reasoning—for example, in arithmetic—are different abilities. Some patients do quite well with hard, identifiable, codable tangibles, but do poorly in concept-formation. Such difficulties perhaps cause thought perseveration, possibly a secondary effect as the mind attempts to hold on to elusive data. These patients often manifest poor organizing abilities and confusions with instructions. A very disturbing problem, especially in highschoolers, relates to social malperceptions and poor judgment in interpersonal situations. I'm certain that many secondary emotional problems arise. Yet I wonder whether the poor social judgment might have been caused originally by poor message processing and disorganized cognitions as described above.

As for disorders of language, speech, and hearing, some children, even though they hear well in testing situations, still have impaired discrimination of auditory stimuli. They have trouble, for example, distinguishing between "tub" and "tug" or between "pit" and "pick" or between "gun" and "bun." Diagnostic tests and norms for guidance are available.

I feel that one of the most intriguing areas of development has to do with language—language dysfunction as opposed to peripheral articulating difficulties in the motoric production of speech. The pathological processes involved, for example, in the dysphasias and aphasias have to do with decoding and encoding problems and with receptive and expressive dysfunctions. There are many conflicting points of view in the many books that have been written on these subjects.

Language delay is one of those symptom-complexes which brings patients to our clinic before school age. Language performance (language competence is difficult to measure) is often equated with normal development and even intelligence. And so, if appropriate language milestones are not achieved at the "correct" ages, parents begin to worry. The differential diagnosis is somewhat involved, but I'd like to mention several interesting points. We must be sure that the patient can hear. Environmental stimulation, "inter-sib language," and especially "twins' language" have to be considered. By appropriate testing, we try to determine whether the language delay is developmentally unique or if there are other slowed areas: for example, large muscle movements, small-muscle coordination, social-personal-adaptive talents. Again, long-term observation and intermittent evaluations are preferable to one-shot assessments.

A fascinating psycholinguisitc concept should be presented and this is that language might well be an innate genetically derived species-specific function of being human rather than a function of being smart. It is true, of course, that vocabulary building, for example, can be taught and learned by environmental stimulation. But there's a good bit of evidence, which makes for exciting reading, that the rules of language (and there seem to be language universals for all the human dialects on earth) are built into us and that not much environmental stimulation is necessary for these potentials to mature, unless pathological processes exist.

This brings us to another provocative thought: there is increasing evidence that there are successive stages in normal language development just as there are such stages in skeletal, motoric, and cognitive (the work of Jean Piaget) maturations. By painstaking, longitudinal observations and recordings, psycholinguistic researchers have determined that, for example, negative, interrogative, and active-passive grammatical transformations become evident in a child's speech (and in his underlying language) within certain relatively specific ages.

A word about *histidinemia*, a rare inherited metabolic deficiency of the enzyme histidase: it causes language and speech problems, but usually not retardation.

As for dyscalculia, we have discussed these arithmetic problems—at least three subtypes—in a previous chapter.

A funny thing happened at our house today. My Lawfully-Wedded, in a fit of guilt or one of pique (I hadn't paid too much attention to her) decided to tidy up and dust my library. Well, you know the note cards that were strewn about had been put there not at random but by design. And when the dust was lifted and the note cards finally settled back on my desk, floor, and lampshade, that design was undone and this book set back by some eight hours—a good time to break so that I can reorganize.

Dyslexia
Dysgraphia
Dysspellia

Can See...Can Hear...
No Gross Neurological Problem...
No Primary Emotional Disturbance...
General I.Q. Within Normal Limits...
Adequate Educational Opportunity...

"Kid, you gotta loin good Inglish— udderwise you ain't never gonna get nowhere!"*

DYSLEXIA, DYSGRAPHIA AND DYS-SPELLIA —
(Remember you saw it *here first*.)

Dyslexia (developmental, primary) is a specific difficulty in learning to read, often genetically determined, which exists despite a level of general intelligence which is at least average. Developmental dyslexia is without obvious brain pathology, without significant impairment of hearing or vision, initially without resistance to conventional instruction methods, and *originally* without emotional disturbance.

Ours is a society that places high value on scholastic achievement. In great part, we tend to equate eventual socioeconomic success with academic accomplishment. This is manifested in the early years of schooling by a heavy emphasis on reading. Teachers of the early school years indicate that if the child can read at grade level, then academically there is little to fear. If a child is not reading at grade level, the possibilities of lower track placement, remedial reading, or even retention in grade for a year of "catching up" present themselves. To get a youngster to read at grade level is a constant goal for teachers, a worry for parents, and a confusion for students. Despite all this attention, however, it is estimated that at least 10% of all children in the United States are handicapped by reading incompetence before they reach the seventh grade (R. Rabinovitch, "Reading Problems in Children," in Keeney and Keeney, editors, *Dyslexia*. St. Louis, C. V. Mosby Co., 1968.) Among professionals in this area, an ac-

---

*From *Classic Expressions I Have Known and Loved.*

cepted definition of reading incompetence is "a significant discrepancy between the actual reading level and the expected reading level for performance mental age." Considered as *significant* is one year's reading delay in children up to ten years of age and two year's delay in children older than ten.

About one-fourth to one-third of all children with reading incompetence probably have primary developmental dyslexia. The rest of the children belong to a secondary category: their problems are usually caused by a lack of motivation or opportunity. Rarely do children develop dyslexia as a result of definitive acquired cerebral lesions or psychopathology. There is little doubt, as attested by many workers in the field, that if psychopathology is not indeed an *initial* factor in the development of dyslexia, it soon assumes secondary (but nonetheless great) importance in an already complicated problem. This is because of the pressures to read and the problems that soon arise out of an inability to do so.

Even though no specific personality aberrations characterize the dyslexic who has suffered emotional trauma as a result of being categorized as mentally hazy, emotionally crazy, and/or motivationally lazy, certain reaction patterns have been noted. Macdonald Critchley (*The Dyslexic Child*, Springfield, Ill., Charles C Thomas, 1970) has indicated that compensatory maneuvers include attempts at excelling in nonliterate skills—for example, in sports. Or, unfortunately, because of the loss of self-esteem the dyslexic at times permits himself to develop into the classroom clown. The tribulations these children must undergo, including academic problems, are seen in social situations as well. Difficulties and subsequent stresses are noted in attempting to read menus, programs, road signs, and newspaper articles, and in the inability to correspond by letter. Many dyslexics, in addition to being unable to organize graphic symbols to make cognitive sense, also have trouble arranging graphic symbols on paper, the cognitions for which are quite clear in their own minds (dysgraphia).

Figure 3 is an example of a dictation exercise given to a seventeen-year-old young man with an average general IQ. His reading teacher was quite puzzled. When she read *The Time Machine* by H. G. Wells to him, our patient understood the characters well, comprehended the plot without any difficulty, and was able to discuss the theme in depth and with insight. Yet he could not read the book by himself! Figure 4 indicates the possible source of his problem. He was first presented *visually* with

Figure 3
Dictation of Dyslexic, Dysgraphic Youngster with Average IQ

DICTATION

1. *the spone wose fole of sugr !*
   The spoon was full of sugar.

2. *the pen youse ink to right wight.*
   The pen uses ink to write with.

3. *the phasadent lives in wastingtone DC*
   The President lives in Washington, D.C.

4. *the p pinsl wich was yello was on the tabl*
   The pencil which was yellow was on the table.

5. *the cup was fad foded cabfe ful of*
   The cup was filled with coffee.

6. *He saip maill thru the strao*
   He sipped milk through the straw.

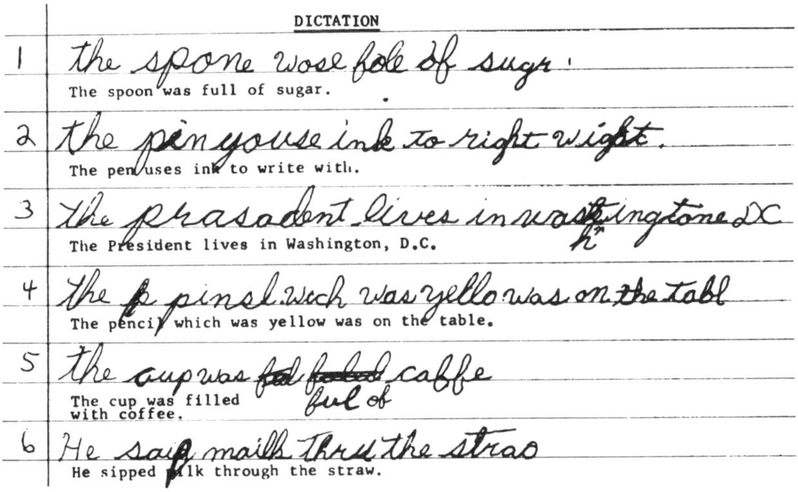

Figure 4
Spelling of Dyslexic, Dysgraphic Youngster with Average IQ

1 - *son spoon*
2 - *g flit pen*
3 - *g yello penol*
4 - *cup*
5 - *strio*

VISUALLY PRESENTED OBJECTS

1 SPooN - *spoon*
2 PEN - *pen*
3 PENCIL - *pencil*
4 CUP - *cup*
5 STRAW - *strau*

COPYING FROM PRINTED MATERIAL

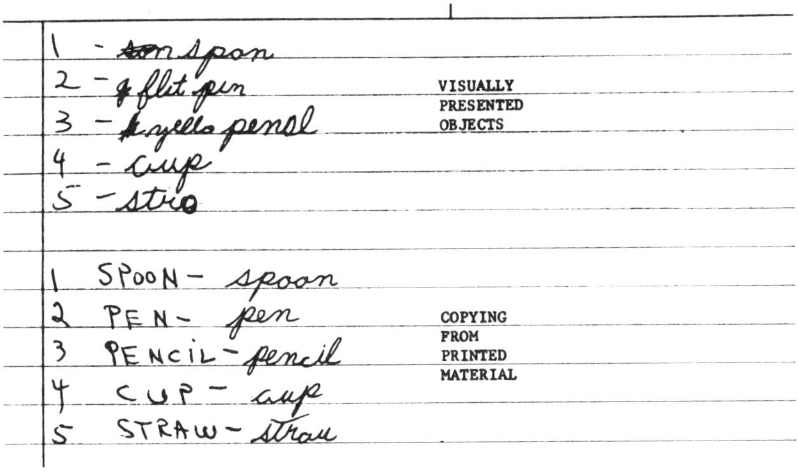

several common objects—spoon, felt pen, yellow pencil, cup, and straw. He knew their names and functions, yet couldn't write their names acceptably on paper. (Please note that there really is no problem here in small-muscle coordination.) But when he was asked "merely" to copy the same words, no problem. When the maneuver was cognitive-motor, not so OK. When it was visual-visual, OK. My first job was to convince this young man that he wasn't stupid. Luckily he really didn't feel stupid, although he was puzzled as to why he couldn't read. My second job was to explain what dyslexia/dysgraphia/dys-spellia is. Part of my explanation included showing dictation examples of others (without names) and mentioning famous men who had the same problems. It is interesting to note that some of our patients do much better on this dictation with a typewriter. Perhaps the neural connections (synapses) between brain and finger and typewriter key are different from connections between brain and finger and pencil. Two poignant and related statements by two patients stand out in my mind:

> "My writing makes fabulous reading."
> "Whenever I sound it out, it's wrong."

Figures 5, 6, 7, and 8 are examples of the dictation of a Mexican-American man who has an average IQ, who speaks quite well in both languages (he's a member of a speaking club), and yet has trouble reading and writing English and Spanish. It is in-

Figure 5
Dictation of Bilingual, Dyslexic, Dysgraphic Adult
with Average IQ (English)

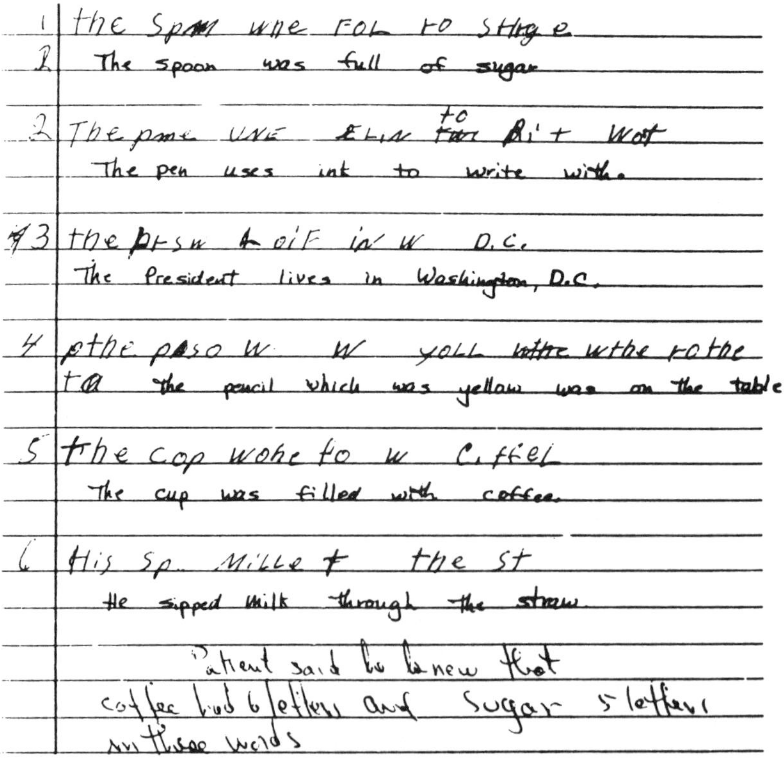

1.	*Sr*	(straw)	
2.	*pmpon*	(pen)	
3.	*pasc*	(pencil)	Visually
4.	*svoand*	(spoon)	Presented
5.	*Cop*	(cup)	Objects
6.			
7.			
8.			
1.	STRAW	StRAW	
2.	PEN	PEN	Copying from
3.	PENCIL	PENCIL	Printed Material
4.	SPOON	SPOON	
5.	CUP	Cup	

teresting, as a compensatory mechanism perhaps, that our patient indicated (Figure 5) that he knew that "coffee" had six letters and "sugar" five. To be as accurate as possible, the same dictation was given in Spanish (Figures 7 and 8). He had the same difficulties. Looking back on it, I can see a few errors on my part: "pipa" is not really a good translation for "straw." And as seen in Figure 8 at the bottom, in a moment of forgetfulness I neglected to translate "cup" and "spoon" into Spanish. Also, purists might say that my Judaico-New York accent confused our patient in both the English and Spanish dictation. But I suppose if one de-designs a scientific experiment with too much rigor, it takes all the fun out of it. Clinical research by its very nature is a bit different from research in the experimental laboratory. Also, the more rigor we put into a clinical experimental design, the closer perhaps we come (both spellingly and semantically) to rigor mortis.

Figure 7

**Dictation of Bilingual, Dyslexic, Dysgraphic Adult
with Average IQ (Spanish)**

Dictation

1. LASi S   Or O   Sr
   La cuchora esta llena de azucar.

2. P   Sr +   P S
   La pluma usa tinta para escribir.

3. L   P V And W   DC
   El Presidente vive en Washington, D. C.

4. L S K R   M   S   N   L M
   El lapiz, que era amarillo estoba en la mesa.

5. LN   Sr   C   L Ki=
   La copa estoba llena con cafe.

6. LF LA I   Los peA
   El bebía leche por la pipa.

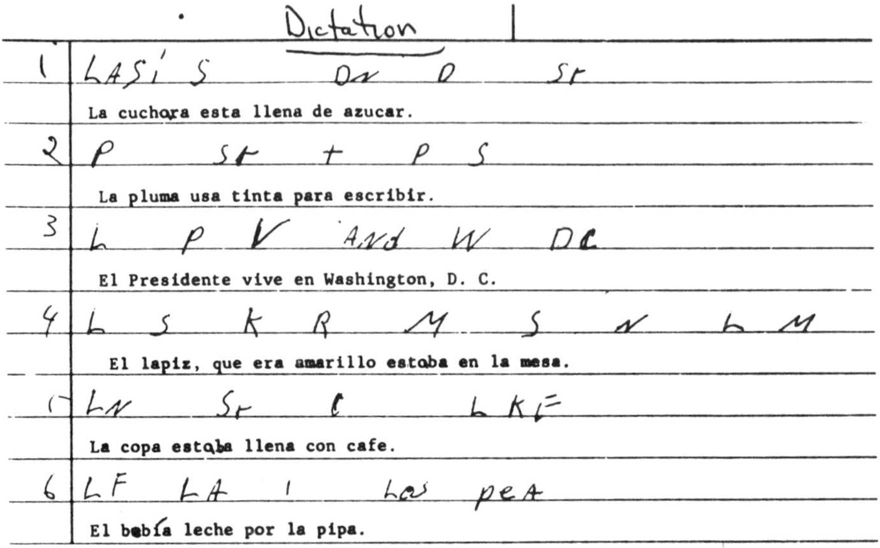

Figure 8

**Spelling of Bilingual, Dyslexic, Dysgraphic Adult
with Average IQ (Spanish)**

1 - p
2 -Lp S
3 -PM   Visually presented objects.
4 - C
5 -Lp

1 PIPA   - PiPA
2 LAPIZ - LAPiZ
3 PLUMA - PLUMA   Copying from printed material
4 CUP   - CUP
5 SPOON - SPOON

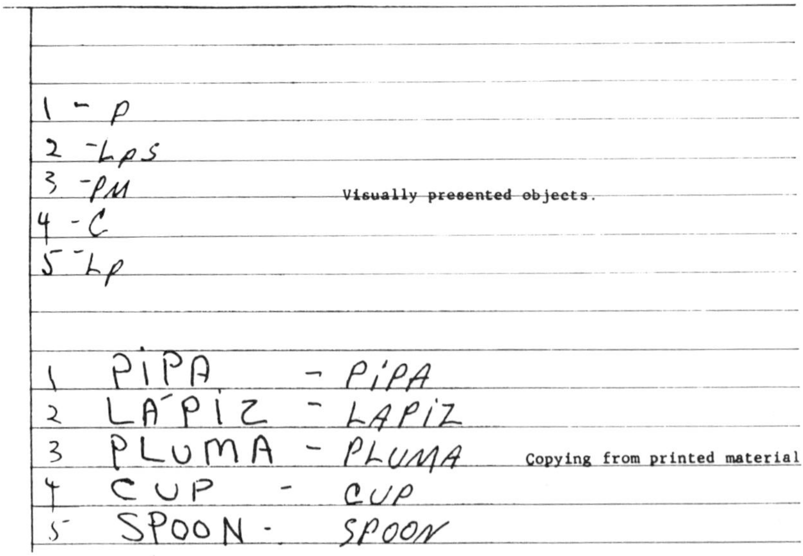

The more general intelligence a dyslexic has, the harder it is
for him to understand or accept his academic lagging behind

younger siblings and peers. Another great problem for the dys-lexic is the diminution of information flow, which causes him to rely heavily on auditory and pictorial information, a compensatory method which is at times quite well developed. A therapeutic measure that exploits the auditory ability is *Talking Books* —records for dyslexics, as well as for the blind, that can be ordered from the Library of Congress, Division for the Blind and Physically Handicapped. (I must here admit to a goof which points out the exquisite sensitivity these youngsters develop. Because I hadn't properly explained *Talking Books* to one boy, he refused them. On the record player were the words "For the Blind.")

An unfortunate reaction which dyslexics show at times is aggression. Macdonald Critchley (*The Dyslexic Child*, Springfield, Ill., Charles C Thomas, 1970) quotes the work of Edmond Critchley, who in 1968 studied the possibility of a correlation between dyslexia and juvenile delinquency. He investigated the incidence of reading disability in a Remand Home and Classifying Centre for the twelve Inner London boroughs. In a group of 106 delinquent boys studied prospectively and 371 retrospectively, ranging in age from twelve to seventeen years, he found that 60% were delayed in reading by two years or more, and 50% by over three years. Probably a good many had reading problems because of socio-motivational factors. However, some almost certainly had primary developmental dyslexia. Nonetheless, there seemed to be a high correlation between acted-out antisocial aggression and problems in reading.

Samuel T. Orton, (*Reading, Writing and Speech Problems in Children*, New York, W. W. Norton, 1937) in his classic work on reading, writing, and speech problems in children, described emotional and personality disturbances secondary to the social trauma of reading incompetence. These secondary effects include feelings of frustration, inferiority, instability, neuroticism, and rebellious acting-out.

Margaret Rawson (*Developmental Language Disability*, Baltimore, Johns Hopkins, 1968), who has had great clinical and research experience with dyslexics, feels that few of her patients are free of emotional problems such as low self-esteem and personal tension; she also notes that the emotional problems seldom appear to cause learning failures—rather, they are effects. She stresses that problems of low self-esteem in a group of boys were more prevalent and persistent among those who were given help *after* they had experienced failure than among those who were helped *before*. This has been the experience at our learning disabilities clinic. It is difficult for dyslexic students to believe they are able to succeed, as the evidence of their actual intellectual capacity is presented to them.

We recently studied twenty dyslexic boys and learned that they had significantly less self-esteem than control groups of normals and asthmatics. In addition, we divided our dyslexic group into two subgroups of ten boys each:

1. Dyslexia No Mystery (DNM): the family understood the problem because the diagnosis had been made before in another family member or in a close friend.
2. Dyslexia Mystery (DM): the family had no experience or understanding of the term, the problem, and its consequences.

There was significantly lower self-esteem in the Dyslexia Mystery Subgroup than in the Dyslexia No Mystery Subgroup. Our suggestion is that lack of information leads to anxiety and guilt in the family and to low self-esteem in the patients—and probably in the parents, too. In parent interviews later on, it was my feeling that information about dyslexia changed family attitudes—for example, it led to more sympathy and understanding of these troubled children.

When the children are still quite young (grades one, two, and three) or when they are awaiting special remediation classes, I sometimes suggest a tutor. The tutor should be sensitive, should work with the teacher, and must be well liked by the patient— BUT PROBABLY SHOULD NOT BE THE PARENT! There's just too much emotional steam released when one tries to tutor one's own child. *A* parent is OK but not *the* parent. What I mean is that it's not a bad idea for parents with school-troubled youngsters to trade children for tutoring purposes.

The familial aspects of dyslexia are most intriguing. That a perceptual problem can be inherited has been noted in other syndromes as well. John Money ("Visual Constructional Deficit in Turner's Syndrome," *Journal of Pediatrics* 69:126-127, 1966) has written on the visual-constructional deficit in children with Turner's syndrome. In addition to loss of space form, children with Turner's syndrome also have impaired directional sense. In relation to the genetic aspects of dyslexia, substantial research has been done in the Scandinavian countries, where the follow-up has been quite adequate. B. Hallgren ("Specific Dyslexia," *Acta*

Psychologica et Neurologica, Supplement 65, 1-287) has authenticated not only an autosomal dominant type of transmission but also a higher incidence in boys. Hallgren also found that of twelve monozygotic twin pairs with dyslexia, there was a concordance rate of 100%; in the dizygotic twin sets, there was 33% concordance. In addition, Hallgren investigated the importance of the dyslexic child in the birth series. He found after careful investigation that ordinal position was not related to the occurrence of primary developmental dyslexia.

Macdonald Critchley ("Isolation of the Specific Dyslexic," in Keeney and Keeney, editors, *Dyslexia*, St. Louis, C. V. Mosby Co., 1968) has discussed the notion that developmental dyslexia has its greatest incidence in English-speaking cultures, and therefore may well have something to do with the spelling difficulties inherent in the English language. The same is presumably the case with developmental dyslexia in some Scandinavian countries. Critchley believes, however, that this is not the complete explanation. He stresses that although very little is known about the precise geographic distribution of developmental dyslexia, it is known to occur in Italy where the language has an extremely logical spelling and pronunciation. Developmental dyslexia also occurs in Russia and Rumania, where the language is pronounced as it is spelled and spelled as it is pronounced. Critchley feels that analysis of the role of the laterality of the written language would be helped by comparing the incidence of dyslexia in those languages, such as English, in which the print runs from left to right, with the incidence in those that proceed from right to left, such as Arabic, Hebrew, Persian, and Hindi. However, one of Critchley's most interesting patients was a bilingual boy who spoke Arabic and English and was dyslexic in both languages. Another interesting patient was a youngster who was dyslexic in English, French, Latin, Gaelic, and Afrikaans. Critchley does not believe that the individual language or the polyglottism played the important role here; he feels that the dyslexia was innate in the constitutional makeup of the patient. (We have a patient who has an average IQ and speaks fluently but has trouble reading and writing—German, English, Hebrew, and Hungarian.)

Yet some fascinating reports from Japan stress the rarity of reading problems among Japanese children. K. Makita ("The Rarity of Reading Disability in Japanese Children," *American Journal of Orthopsychiatry*, 38:599-614, 1968) feels that the fact that poor readers are extremely rare among Japanese children should be examined from a philological, rather than a physiological, point of view. Makita stresses that English exceeds by far all other Western languages in the number of words in which irregular or unstable relationships exist between spelling and pronunciation or between the grapheme and the phoneme. In this respect, the Japanese *Kana* (syllabic script) stands in extreme contrast to English: in *Kana*, the script-phonetic relationship is almost a key-to-keyhole situation. However, Critchley (*Aphasiology*, London, Edward Arnold, Ltd., 1970) felt that the rarity of dyslexia in Japan is due more to the fact that there are two scripts in Japanese. He notes that in the few cases of dysgraphia reported from Japan, there were fewer involving *Kanji* (ideographic characters) than *Kana*.

The work of Elena Boder, a pediatric neurologist in Los Angeles, should be mentioned as opening up some stunning speculations in the dyslexia-dysgraphia complex—perhaps with specific relation to the cortical areas of localization I have mentioned. There seem to be three subtypes of dyslexia:

Dysphonetic Dyslexia: In this type there are problems in sound-symbol integration. Such dyslexics, because of limited phonics skills, tend to read globally. They have trouble with words not in their sight vocabulary. Their mistakes tend to be nonphonetic, semantic substitution errors: "whole" for "full," "funny" for "laugh," "chicken" for "duck." Such dyslexics could presumably be taught by sight-see methods.

Dyseidetic Dyslexia: In this type the trouble is in not being able to perceive words as wholes or Gestalts. Such dyslexics read phonetically, even words previously encountered. Their misspellings are phonetic, intelligible, and even "cute": "lisn" for "listen," "sos" for "sauce," "laf" for "laugh." Such dyslexics could presumably be taught by phonics methods.

A third group, probably almost alexic, has the problems of the two preceding types.

The best way to end this chapter is to recount some verbal interplay that occurred recently between a patient and myself when I asked for his photograph. I like to have a photograph of each youngster on the chart for recognition when I review case histories:

ME: "Johnny, I'd like to get a picture of you for the chart."
JOHNNY: "Why sure, Doc. Do you have trouble seeing words too?"

Epilogue

And now—nine months after beginning this book—I'm a little happier with the later chapters than with the earlier ones. I'd like to think this has to do with growth—mine.

Did I do what I said I'd do? Looking back to the first chap-chapter, I said I wanted to:

> give information in a very fuzzy area,
>
> pull it all together,
>
> give pleasurable reading.

I hope I did.

Now that my baby is leaving me and going out into a world of critics, I'm not as complacent as when I started. Everyone wants to be liked and respected. I hope I was clear, yet not dogmatic. I hope I was open-minded, but not wishy-washy.

I wanted to be modest and laud the names of the many (all the way back to PS 92 in Manhattan) who were responsible for my educational and philosophical background. This message I got, gently but firmly: "Joe . . . Joe . . . you write in . . . er . . . an unusual style. Let's wait to see if there's a second printing. And *then* you can thank us."

My guilt! What can I say to my lovely wife and my three great sons for the time I spent away from them while writing this book? My middle one approached me once: "Dad . . . could you . . . oh, you're busy . . . I'll catch you later." In the long run, did I do more good or bad? A word about pushing kids.

Vignette

We were picnicking in a small community noted for its intellectuals. Near us, a father was reading to his son . . . who was about four years old . . . with forceful, clear enunciation . . . A Tale of Two Cities . . . A TALE OF TWO CITIES? BY DICKENS? . . . Yup! I know because I remembered the parts from the movie . . . I really don't think you should push kids before they're ready . . . I cuddled my then two-year-old. . . . For two balloons and a candy bar, he looked straight ahead . . . and I read from an imaginery book . . . Gallia Est Omnis Divisa In Partes Tres . . . it was all I could remember (since I had never studied it) . . . but it was Caesar's Gallic Wars—in Latin yet! . . . The other Dad heard, winced, smiled funny-like, shook his head, and walked away. . . . A little later, over the short-wave radio, we heard a May Day call for a psychiatrist . . . this Dad was walking about dazed and mumbling . . . "But he read to him in Latin yet . . . but he read to him in Latin yet."

We really shouldn't push our kids. Once in an outburst of exuberant liberalism I lined up my three boys and said, "You guys can be any type of . . . *doctors* . . . you want to be!"

As I let the manuscript slip through my fingers for the final return-receipt-requested-mail-run to the editor, I think:

"Have I offended anyone?"

"Have I offended myself?"

I hope not.

I'm Not Distractible!!...
I'm Distracted!!...